Cornell

Alice Miller lives in Switzerland, where for more than twenty years she taught and practised psychoanalysis. Now, she radically questions the validity of psychoanalytic theories and psychiatric methods. Her books include *The Drama of Being a Child*; *For Your Own Good: Hidden Cruelty in Child-rearing and the Roots of Violence*; *Thou Shalt Not Be Aware: Society's Betrayal of the Child*; and *Pictures of a Childhood*. In the autumn of 1990 Virago will publish her important new work on therapy, *Banished Knowledge: Facing Childhood Injuries*.

ALICE MILLER

TRANSLATED FROM
THE GERMAN BY
HILDEGARDE AND
HUNTER HANNUM

*Tracing
Childhood
Trauma
in
Creativity
and
Destructiveness*

VIRAGO

THE UNTOUCHED KEY

Published by VIRAGO PRESS Limited 1990
20–23 Mandela Street, Camden Town, London NW1 0HQ

Translation copyright © Alice Miller 1990

All rights reserved

A CIP catalogue record for this book is available from the British Library

Originally published as *Der gemiedene Schlüssel* by Suhrkamp Verlag am
Main, copyright © 1988. Any variations from the original German text
are a result of the author's wishes.

FRONTISPIECE: Picasso, *Guernica*
                1990 ARS N.Y./SPADEM

Printed in Great Britain by Cox & Wyman Ltd., Reading, Berks

Contents

Preface   *vii*

PART ONE   *Repressed Childhood Experiences*
              in Art   *1*

  1 Pablo Picasso: The Earthquake in Málaga
     and the Painter's Eye of a Child   *3*

  2 Käthe Kollwitz: A Mother's Dead Little
     Angels and Her Daughter's Activist Art   *19*

  3 Buster Keaton: Laughter at a Child's
     Mistreatment and the Art of Self-Control   *37*

  4 Despot or Artist?   *47*

PART TWO   *Friedrich Nietzsche: The Struggle*
              Against the Truth   *71*

  A Mistreated Child, a Brilliant Mind,
  and Eleven Years of Darkness   *73*

PART THREE *The No Longer Avoidable*
                Confrontation with Facts   *135*
  1 When Isaac Arises from the Sacrificial
     Altar   *137*
  2 The Emperor's New Clothes   *147*

Appendix   The Newly Recognized, Shattering
                Effects of Child Abuse   *167*
Notes   *171*
Bibliography   *176*
Acknowledgments   *179*

Preface

*W*henever I leaf through a biography of a creative person, I find information on the first pages of the book that is especially helpful in my work. The information has to do with one or more childhood events whose traces are always apparent in the person's creative work, usually running through it like a continuous thread. In spite of this, the individual childhood events usually are not given any prominence by the biographer. The facts surrounding them could be likened to a key ring we have found but have no use for. We don't know who the owner is, and we suspect the person has long since moved to another house and therefore will no longer have the slightest interest in the lost keys.

Is it permissible, then, for me to take these keys and try to match them to the doors of old houses to discover a life that has long been waiting to be recognized? It may be considered indiscreet to open the doors of someone else's house and rummage around in other people's family histories. Since so many of us still have the tendency to idealize our parents, my undertaking may even be regarded as improper. And yet it is something that I think must be done, for the amazing knowledge that comes to light from behind those previously locked doors contributes substantially toward helping people rescue themselves from their dangerous sleep and all its grave consequences.

ONE

Repressed Childhood Experiences in Art

1

PABLO PICASSO:
The Earthquake in Málaga and the Painter's Eye of a Child

*T*he throngs of people at the exhibit of Picasso's late works in Basel make it difficult to get a good look at the pictures. Groups of students are being told by experts how they should interpret Picasso. They are trying hard to understand something they could learn about just as well at home from Picasso reproductions—for example, his skill in composition. Many of them yawn, turn away from the pictures, look at their watches, and probably think of the cup of coffee that will come to their rescue. The expert who is instructing them doesn't give up; he tries the theory of color, explaining how the orange makes the blue stand out and how well Picasso knew which colors to use for a strong effect. This too seems to bore the students. They are making a visible effort to take in what their instructor is saying and to be sure not to forget it, but the Picasso who is being explained here is somehow dead, one artist among others who have great skill and a mastery of color and form.

Yet along with the many bored and yawning faces, I think I can detect some that are curious, fascinated, and disquieted. I myself feel something like gratitude for this great festival of color I am permitted to feast my eyes on and for Picasso's courage, from which I take inspiration. This man, nearly ninety when he painted these pictures, disregarded all convention as well as his own technical ability and attained what he had wished for all his life: the spontaneity and freedom of a child, which his perfection-ism robbed him of in childhood.

It may have been precisely this inspiring power of Picasso's late works that helped me gradually forget the great crowds of bored people around me until finally I was fully able to enter inwardly on this adventure. I seemed to be sensing a man's last strenuous efforts to express the most hidden secrets of his life with every means at his disposal before it's too late, before death takes the brush from his hand.

A great deal has been written about the sexual themes in Picasso's work, and they have always been understood as a sign of his virility. The fact that he depicted male and female genital organs with increasing frequency as he grew older, even right up to his death, has been attributed to his declining libido and a longing for pleasures no longer attainable. But anyone who makes the effort to discover the emotional content of Picasso's last pictures of nude men and women will probably sense a sorrow that is much deeper and whose roots reach back much further in Picasso's life than can be explained by an aging man's regrets at his waning sexual vitality.

But what is the origin of his suffering? I asked myself as I walked through the exhibit, and at first I found no answer. I sensed his suffering not only in the themes but also in the force of the brush movements, in the vehement way he sometimes applied the color and conjured up new feelings that had to be given form. I had the impression that these paintings express a struggle between what Picasso *must* do and what he *is able* to do, between the necessity of making these strokes and no other, of using this color and no other, and a highly conscious, masterful eye that cannot unlearn the laws of color theory and composition even if it would like to. The force of necessity increases with such intensity in Picasso's late works that his ability becomes secondary. Feeling is no longer given a shape, as it was in the painting *Guernica*; now it is lived and becomes pure expression. He no longer does drawings, he no longer counts on the viewer's comprehension; there remains only his haste to produce the unsayable, to say it with colors. But what was the unsayable for Picasso?

I viewed the exhibit of his late works with this question in mind and found no answer. I leafed through an endless number of Picasso biographies, searching for trau-

matic experiences in his childhood. Since the efficiency of
defense mechanisms decreases in old age, since repression
works with less ingenuity, it was possible, I thought, that
traces of childhood trauma not evident before might become
visible in his late works. But at first such traces were
undetectable; here was a child who was loved, who had a
happy home life. . . .

Even though I know that biographers are seldom interested in their subjects' childhood, I nevertheless found
it astonishing that in so many books about such a famous
man of our time there was very little—and always the
same—information about Picasso's first years: he was born
in 1881 in Málaga; his father taught drawing; his mother
loved him above all else; at the age of ten he moved to
Barcelona; at age fourteen he entered an art school in
Madrid and was the best student there; when he was seventeen, his father gave him his palette and stopped painting. This chronology is repeated in all the biographies.
Then events that took place in the Spain of that day and
in the rest of the world are described in great detail. The
financial difficulties of his forebears are also thoroughly
discussed, but Pablo Picasso the child is scarcely to be
found. The biography by Josep Palau i Fabre was the only
one in which I found a few pages that could give me some
insight into Picasso's childhood. Although the facts were
scattered here and there, with time they took on meaning
and revealed the logical connections I was looking for. I
read with amazement, for example, about Picasso's behavior in school:

It appears that Picasso's reluctance to go to school was so great that it finally caused him to fall really ill. The doctor said that he had an infection of the kidneys and could not continue to attend classes in that dank building. This news was received with great enthusiasm by little Pablo, for he thought that it meant he would never have to go to school again. And even at the fairly ripe age of eighty-six, Picasso told me that he could never remember the sequence of the alphabet and could not understand how he had ever learned to read and write—or, above all, to count.

When we look back on this childhood situation from the perspective of a famous painter, it seems understandable that the monotonous routine of school would not meet the needs of a child of genius. But it is not that simple. It may be that an alert child is not interested in the multiplication tables or in lists of spelling words because he has already mastered them, whereas the other children are still having trouble. But Picasso *was* having difficulty learning his *ABC*'s. The description of his behavior in school indicates that something entirely different was bothering him. But what?

I continued reading and learned that a second sister was born when he was six and was just starting school. This in itself need not cause problems in school, one might argue, for his mother idolized him and his father was extraordinarily supportive. But what did the birth of his second sister mean for Pablo? Could this event have reminded him of an earlier one? One would have to know the conditions surrounding the birth of his first sister, I thought. I continued my search and was amazed when I found the answer. How is it possible, I wondered, that these facts did not find their way into all the Picasso books, that they were never linked to *Guernica*? Palau i Fabre writes:

> One evening in mid-December 1884—when Picasso was just three years old—there was an earthquake in Málaga. Don José was chatting with some friends in the room behind the local chemist's shop when he saw the rows of jars on the shelves crashing to the floor. The party broke up immediately, its members hastening to their various homes. Don José was in his apartment in a very few moments and said to his wife: "These rooms are too big, María: get dressed quickly! And you, Pablo, come along with me."
>
> Picasso's own account of this incident, as told to Sabartés, went as follows: "My mother was wearing a kerchief on her head: I had never seen her like that before. My father took his cloak from its hanger, flung it over his shoulders, snatched me up and wrapped me in its folds until only my head was peeping out."
>
> They then left the apartment and went to Muñoz Degrain's house, at No. 60 in the Calle de la Victoria. . . .
>
> The Calle de la Victoria, which is one of the longest streets in Málaga, runs parallel to the western slope of the hill of Gibralfaro. It does not exactly lean on this slope, as has been said, but almost certainly the foundations of its houses are set upon the rocky outcrops of the hill. This was the explicit reason that led Don José to seek a refuge for his family in that house. Muñoz Degrain himself was away from home at the time, having gone to Rome on a painting trip with Moreno Carbonero.

A few days after moving into this temporary home—on 28th December 1884, to be precise, according to the attached birth certificate—the couple's second child was born, a girl who was given the name Lola (the most usual diminutive of Dolores). . . .

The earthquake that led to the family's removal must have been quite a considerable one, for a few days later King Alfonso XII visited Málaga to see the extent of the damage for himself.

I didn't find the exact date of the earthquake in any of the numerous biographies, but after making some telephone inquiries I finally learned that on December 25, 1884, Spain was shaken by a severe earthquake, with six seismic shocks occurring between nine and eleven at night. The epicenter was in Arenas del Rey, less than twenty miles from Málaga. Many years later Picasso told his friend Sabartés: " 'My father thought it safer to be near the rocks.' " Sabartés himelf adds, "There [the family] spent anxious days waiting for the earth to settle." Picasso's sister was born three days after the earthquake; possibly labor was induced by the fright his mother experienced. So in the space of three days the three-year-old Picasso had to cope with the shock of an earthquake and the birth of his first sister in a highly unusual situation and in strange surroundings.

This example made clear to me once again how fruitless historical research can be if the psychological significance of external events is not taken into consideration simply because an adult is rarely able to understand the feelings of a child. Just try to imagine what it must be like for a three-year-old to have his father take him and his pregnant mother through the dark city during an earthquake to a strange house and then to be present at the birth of his sister. In Picasso's case two additional factors were at work: being encouraged to see by his father and being told to be silent by his mother. As a little boy, he began to perfect his way of seeing, but he was not supposed to put what he saw into words. All his life, Picasso was proud of his "discretion," the result of his mother's warning—one of his earliest memories—"not to say anything about anybody or anything."

Picasso's mother liked to tell people that her son could draw before he could walk. His first word was *piz*, one of whose meanings in Spanish is "pencil" in baby talk. His father took the greatest pleasure in the little boy's progress in drawing, a fact that surely did not escape the son's notice. When he was drawing, Pablo no doubt received the most attention and encouragement from his father, attention that in an otherwise female household was naturally very important. His father's fondest wish was for his son to win the recognition as a painter that he himself, to his sorrow, had never been given. And the son's wish was for his father to love him.

By the age of three, Picasso was already drawing from his father's models; in particular he drew doves. This taught the boy to look very carefully, to observe an object closely, and to distinguish among the variety of forms. The earlier a child masters something, the more deeply it becomes imprinted and the more certain he is of success for the rest of his life. This is why, conversely, negative messages and experiences are so difficult to unlearn.

Picasso had just turned three in October 1884. What happens to a child who has learned so well at such an early age to use his eyes, to observe his surroundings very closely and register every change, when he is subjected to as terrible a trauma as an earthquake? Perhaps his poem about Spain, written in 1936, can give us a faint idea:

> Children's screams screams of women bird screams flower screams screams of beams and stones screams of bricks screams of furniture of beds of chairs of curtains of frying pans of cats and of papers screams of smells that scrape at one another screams of smoke that burns in the throats of the screams cooking in the pot and screams of raining birds who flood the sea which gnaws the bone that breaks its teeth . . .

Because I saw in these words the verbal and in *Guernica* the visual portrayal of an earthquake as experienced by a child, I thought my discovery would have to be equally exciting for others. But I was mistaken. Picasso experts said that it had happened too long ago and that biography had no significance for the work of such a great painter. Again and again, I am deeply affected by facts that do not count for others—at first. But years later, when resistance has somehow been weakened, it occasionally happens that what was once so vehemently disputed is then taken for granted by others too.

We don't know precisely what was taking place on the Calle de la Victoria as little Pablo was being carried down the long street by his father, but we have a good idea. No doubt the boy saw horses lying in the street, contorted faces, children wandering around; he must have heard terrible screams of fear. Unfortunately, no scholars have yet tried to find out how severe the earthquake in Málaga was, whether houses collapsed as well, and what scenes of human misery and suffering took place before the observant eyes of a child who was later to be a genius. For lack of this information, we can turn to *Guernica*, painted in 1937, in which Picasso portrayed the misery of a war he never was in. He painted the scene in such a way that those who see it can experience their own feelings of horror, terror, and helplessness in the face of total destruction—provided they do not let themselves be distracted by the opinions of art critics. He even painted himself over to the right as the bewildered child in the cellar.

Guernica owes the immediacy of its emotional impact on the viewer, it now strikes me, to Picasso's experiences during the 1884 earthquake in Málaga, experiences that affected his imagination so profoundly that they played an enduring role in his art. The crying, contorted female faces he painted in the period following *Guernica* can even be traced directly in theme to these experiences. He is not attempting to express his own inner state in the faces he paints, as is the case with Edvard Munch in *The Scream* or with various other expressionist painters; rather, Picasso's portrayals are of actual screaming and crying women, but their features cannot be clearly distinguished and their suffering, circumstances, and history are as incomprehensible to us as strangers screaming in the street must be to a child who doesn't know the reason for their terror.

As I looked at Picasso's paintings, I often felt I was seeing with the eyes of the confused, uncomprehending, disoriented, but interested and curious child. We try to distinguish the individual parts of the bodies of his nudes: Where is the foot? Where is the hand? Why are the eyes placed so that they aren't looking at us, so that they can't look at anyone? Art historians tell us that Picasso wanted to show both the front and the back of a head simultaneously because that was part of his "program" at the time. But why? Was Picasso a person who had to adhere to programs? After all, he always abandoned a style once he had developed it, since it bored him to be tied to any one in particular. But the theme of the distorted human body haunted him all his life. It seems to me that his brush was guided by a compulsion he neither understood nor recognized and indeed could not explain because it emerged from his unconscious, which had been imprinted with his earliest childhood experiences. If Picasso had felt constrained to show proof of his ability, he would have stayed with one of his successful phases, perhaps the cubist one. But he had proven his ability long ago when he was still a little boy. Therefore, as an old man he was free to paint what his repressed experience dictated without having to demonstrate his mastery of technique, color, and so on; only then was he able to let what was stored in his unconscious speak through colors.

Little children often express their traumas in a painting the moment a brush is put into their hand. They don't know what they are portraying, and unfortunately adults are practiced in overlooking the revealing content of children's art. Picasso, however, did not have the opportunity to express himself spontaneously as a child; he said that he always painted grown-up pictures, and it took forty years before he was able to paint like a child, that is, to let his unconscious speak. In the same way that adults often are deaf to the cry for help expressed in a child's drawing, taking pleasure instead in the pretty colors and broad strokes, the public received Picasso's later, incomprehensible works with favor, for he was, after all, already recognized as a master.

One can, if one must, see the twisted, distorted female nudes still being done by the artist at ninety simply as a sign of his preoccupation with sex. I prefer to picture the three-year-old boy who, in the midst of all the turmoil of the earthquake and the family's flight, was also witness to his sister's birth. Even if the adults had thought the boy might be traumatized, an awareness of psychology that would not have been likely in those days, probably in the family's temporary quarters no one could have kept this lively, curious child from witnessing the event around which everything now revolved. How does a woman giving birth look from the perspective of a three-year-old, and what happens in the young boy's psyche when this woman writhing in pain happens to be his mother? And all this in surroundings that have just been rocked by an earthquake. The little boy had to repress his feelings, but many images no doubt remained fixed in his memory, although separated from their context.

It is an open question how much viewers can recognize of these events of early childhood in Picasso's paintings. Such awareness should by no means be made into an obligatory program. I want only to indicate that even as severe a trauma as an earthquake need not be repressed entirely but can be represented in works of art if the traumatized child experienced his parents' love and protection when the catastrophe occurred. In addition, I want to point out how much we miss if we disregard the dimension of early childhood experience.

The artist is left with his loneliness as the child was with his: posterity does not concern itself with his trauma but only with his achievement. His paintings can bring in high prices the same way his childhood accomplishments brought him high praise. The more his pictures are praised, however, the more the artist who painted them remains alone with his truth, as I sensed so clearly at the exhibit in Basel. An earthquake in Málaga in 1884? Who cares about that today? Witness to the birth of his sister? What's so unusual about that? But if we put everything together —the earthquake and the birth, the plight of his parents and of the whole city, an upbringing of seeing but remaining silent—a particular constellation emerges that was of indelible significance for this particular individual, Pablo Picasso. Had Picasso not been carried along the Calle de la Victoria in the arms of the father he loved, he might have become psychotic or he might have had to repress the trauma so totally that he would have become an upstanding, compulsive functionary in Franco's Spain. Then it would have been no coincidence if he had taken a special interest in the production of weapons capable of destroying whole cities in one blow.

His father's sheltering arms made it possible for the little boy to overcome his terrifying experience in an optimal manner. Thanks to this protective care, he was able to store what he saw in a way that permitted him to keep expressing it in new forms in his art. Thus, he escaped psychosis as well as total emotional self-alienation (which characterizes the life of so many people) even though he suffered a severe trauma not only at the age of three but even at birth. Most biographers report major complications connected with Picasso's birth. "Apparently, Picasso had such a difficult birth that he was at first thought to be stillborn. Such was evidently the opinion of the midwife, at any rate, for she left him lying on a table in order to devote her attention to his mother. It was only thanks to the presence of mind shown by his doctor uncle, Don Salvador, that the baby came to life." Thus, Picasso, like so many babies, was deprived at birth of being held in his mother's arms, of finding comfort and reassurance there after surviving the struggle for life, and of storing up tenderness and a feeling of trust at this crucial moment. But the later affection shown by his parents, aunts, and cousins helped him to keep taking anew the step leading from death to life. Many of Picasso's contemporaries and friends report that he felt wholly alive only when he was painting. Only then was it possible for him to escape the lethal compulsion to achieve and instead to taste the freedom of inspiration, feeling, and impulse—that is, of life.

The three-year-old Picasso was painfully reminded of the trauma of his own birth by the horrors of the earthquake, the proximity of death, *and* the birth of his sister. But these shocks to his psyche subsided, since the boy's home life was happy and he was permitted to play. It was the discipline and constraints he experienced in school that reawakened his fears, especially since another birth, that of his second sister just as he was starting school, reminded him of his earlier trauma. This highly intelligent child at first reacted to school with learning problems and a severe illness, but as a result of the love and support of his family he did not succumb. He was allowed to rebel against the stultifying constraints confronting him and, even in the Spain of that day, succeeded in expressing his needs.

When taken to school Pablo always demanded, especially from his father, some sort of pledge or token; and quite frequently this was the pigeon he used as a model. And the teacher . . . was quite willing to let him keep this pigeon on his desk and draw it to his heart's content. Nevertheless, the little boy had such an independent character that whenever he felt inspired to do so he would leave his place, walk over to the window, and tap on the glass on the off-chance of being noticed by somebody who might get him out. His uncle by marriage, Antonio Suárez Pizarro (the husband of Don José's sister Eloisa Ruiz Blasco), since he lived opposite the school, used to keep an eye open for these appearances and would call for his nephew after *one* hour. This figure—one—seemed to Picasso, according to what he had been taught, to be the smallest possible unit, which was why he insisted on it. But how long the waiting felt, how long an hour could seem!

Even today, one hundred years later, parents still believe they must teach their little children discipline, for if the children are already used to being obedient, then they supposedly won't have to "suffer" in school. It is fortunate that there are some children, like Picasso, who do not submit when confronted with rigidity because they haven't experienced it at home. Pablo's revolt against his school harmed no one, even if it did cause headaches for a few adults. It was the first step on the artist's long journey leading away from constricting conventions to the freedom to create, to think, and to feel.

2

KÄTHE KOLLWITZ:
A Mother's Dead Little Angels and Her Daughter's Activist Art

The following observations are a result of my participation in a discussion about Käthe Kollwitz in conjunction with an exhibit of her works in Zurich in 1981. She is not a painter who moves me deeply enough that I would have felt compelled on my own to become involved with her art. For me, the political effect and power of a work do not depend on its conscious themes. Some pictures can arouse my anger, can give me a feeling of wanting to resist or take action without their having to be regarded as political. In the case of Käthe Kollwitz, on the other hand, when I look at her pictures I am inclined to see hopelessness and despair but not a powerful political statement.

Käthe Kollwitz, Vienna Is Dying! Save Her Children!
VAGA New York 1989

But now that I had told the Kunsthaus, the museum where her works were on display, that I would take part in the discussions, I tried to figure out why I found her pictures so depressing (as well as expressive of depression) and why a mother mourning over her dead child appeared so frequently in them. Art historians find what they consider adequate explanations for this, but I was not convinced. They emphasize, for example, that as a doctor's wife, the painter was often confronted with the tragedy of mothers losing their children. In addition, she herself lost her son Peter in 1914 just a few days after he had gone to war as a volunteer, which had been a matter of great pride to her.

Yet Käthe Kollwitz had already been obsessed with the theme of death and the dead child in the arms of its mother long before the death of her son. Simple causality was therefore not the answer, and yet I didn't want to exclude her personal fate as the explanation. I began asking myself how these facts related to one another and whether they might gain new significance if they were placed in a larger, more comprehensive context.

Before turning to Käthe Kollwitz's childhood memories contained in her diaries, I walked through the exhibit and was attentive to the content of her work and its effect on me. Again and again I saw a dead child or a figure of death coming to take the child away from its mother or of death as lover, comforter, or friend who snatches the mother from her terrified children. I also saw death depicted as violently assaulting the children. Then I saw sad figures, prisoners bound with ropes, and revolutionaries whose faces very rarely expressed anger but rather resignation and hopelessness.

I left the exhibit with many unanswered questions. What kind of images did the eyes of Käthe Kollwitz the child take in from her surroundings and store up? Who is the bent, lost-looking, depressive woman to be seen in almost all the pictures? It can't be the self-portrait of a painter who was capable of that much expression and who showed such strength in the strokes of her brush. Could it be her mother, who did *not* have this outlet for self-expression? What role did death play in the artist's childhood? What concrete experiences relate to the idea of death as a child pictures it? What riddles were there for the child to solve? With these questions in mind, I finally opened the pages of Käthe Kollwitz's diaries.

The entries about her childhood were very illuminating. Käthe Kollwitz, born Käthe Schmidt in 1867, grew up in Königsberg in a religious sect called the Free Religious Congregation, which had been founded and run by her maternal grandfather, Julius Rupp. After her grandfather's death, Käthe's father took over leadership of the group. His writings plainly show a mixture of naiveté, coerciveness, and scrupulousness. Käthe was raised to follow rules and orders to the letter and to suppress her feelings in the service of religious values, self-control chief among them. Since she was a very alert and high-spirited child, strict measures and severe punishment were required for her upbringing. The artist describes being locked up by herself for a long time as punishment for screaming, with no one coming to talk to her. Once, a night watchman going by on the street even came to the door because he was alarmed by the child's "bawling." As is so often the case, her older siblings adopted the parents' ways and used similar methods to train the younger child.

I do not remember much about my sister Julie at that time. Later Mother told me that Julie had always been a solicitous child. Two years younger than Konrad, she was always trailing along behind her brother to save him from mischief. Even at that early age she had begun her mothering of us which we later so rebelled against.

Once Mother sent the two of us to visit Ernestine Castell. As Julie was preparing to leave with me, she took a lump of sugar out of the box and pocketed it. "What is that for?" Aunt Tina asked. "To cram into Kaethe's mouth if she starts to bawl," Julie answered.

This stubborn bawling of mine was dreaded by everyone. I could bawl so loudly that no one could stand it. There must have been one occasion when I did it at night, because I remember that the night watchman came to see what was the matter. When Mother took me anywhere, she was thankful if the fit did not come over me in the street, for then I would stop dead in my tracks and nothing could persuade me to move on. If the fit came over me at home, my parents would shut me up alone in a room until I had bawled myself to exhaustion. We were never spanked.

Her stored-up rage led to physical symptoms, whose significance no one could be bothered about.

23

Käthe Kollwitz, Death Reaches for the Children
VAGA New York 1989

[My] stomach aches were a surrogate for all physical and mental pains. I imagine my bilious trouble began at that time. I went around in misery for days at a time, my face yellow, and often lay belly down on a chair because that made me feel better. My mother knew that my stomach aches concealed small sorrows, and at such times she would let me snuggle close to her.

Käthe was allowed to snuggle close to her mother as long as she was quiet and behaved herself and above all didn't say anything about what was troubling her. This resulted in loneliness, self-accusations, and depressive moods beginning in childhood.

On the whole I was a quiet, shy child, and nervous as well. Later on, instead of these tantrums of kicking and roaring I had moods that lasted for hours and even days. When in these moods I could not bring myself to use words to communicate with others. The more I saw what a burden I was being to the family, the harder it became for me to emerge from my mood.

I needed to confide in my mother, to confess to her. Since I could not conceive of lying to my mother, or even of being disobedient, I decided to give my mother a daily report on what I had done and felt that day. I imagined that her sharing the knowledge would be a help to me. But she said nothing at all, and so I too soon fell silent.

There is a picture of [my mother] holding on her lap her first child, which was named Julius after my grandfather. This was the "firstborn child, the holy child," and she had lost it, as well as the one born after it. Looking at her picture you can see that she was truly Julius Rupp's daughter and would never let herself give way completely to grief. But although she never surrendered to the deep sorrow of those early days of her marriage, it must have been her years of suffering which gave her for ever after the remote air of a madonna. Mother was never a close friend and good comrade to us. But we always loved her.

Käthe Kollwitz describes her love for her mother as "tender and solicitous." She was often fearful that her mother might "come to some harm," "get lost," "go mad," or die. Sometimes she wished her parents were already dead, "so that it would all lie behind me." It was inevitable, with all her desperate attempts to hold back her true feelings, that she suffered not only from physical symptoms but from psychic ones as well. She writes:

> I don't know just when I began to suffer from nocturnal frights. . . . Nights I was tormented by frightful dreams. . . . Then there was a horrible state I fell into when objects would begin to grow smaller. It was bad enough when they grew larger, but when they grew smaller it was horrifying.
>
> I experienced such states of unfounded fear for many years; even when I was in Munich [in her early twenties] they occurred, but in far feebler form. I constantly had the feeling that I was in an airless room, or that I was sinking or vanishing away.

Her belief in her own guilt and in the value of a strict upbringing for a person's later life would in itself be sufficient to explain the depressive cast to Käthe Kollwitz's pictures. For if a child is forbidden to express her true feelings, observations, and thoughts because only good, kind thoughts that are pleasing to God are permitted, then everything that has no place in this "good" world is relegated to the realm of death. As a child, Käthe Kollwitz often dreamed she was dead; this was because the uncomfortable, intense side of her nature was not allowed to live. Since I regard depression as the consequence of attempts, such as she was subjected to, to smother life, at first I was inclined to interpret the many depictions of death in her graphic work as the symbolic manifestation of her suffering. Gradually, however, it became clear that the theme of death in her art had other sources as well.

Käthe was one of four siblings—Konrad, Julie, Käthe, and Lise—to live beyond childhood. Her mother's first two children died at a very early age. The last-born child, Benjamin, born after Lise, died of meningitis when he was one year old. This information held great significance for me. Experience shows that the death of a child, especially the firstborn, plays a very important role in a mother's life. The birth of every child inevitably awakens or reawakens desires in the parents that somehow are connected to making up for their own childhoods. Either they look to the child to compensate for their not having had good parents ("At last here is someone who will show concern for me, who will treat me with consideration and respect") or to be the child they once were ("Now I shall have someone to whom I can give all that my parents had to deny me").

If the child dies soon after birth, before the parents' expectations are disappointed by the child's desire for autonomy, the mother may idealize her lost child and thereby preserve its central importance for the rest of her life. Often after the death of an infant, there is no real period of mourning that runs its course; instead, the parents' hopes become attached to an "if": if only the child had lived, the parents think, their expectations would have been met. The belief in the fulfillment of all their hopes, originating in their own childhoods, is associated with the memory of this child, whose grave they visit and tend for decades after.

Superhuman, even divine, qualities are attributed to the dead child; at the same time, the other children in the family grow up in the shadow of this cult. They must be dutifully cared for and raised in a way to rid them of their bad behavior and make them acceptable in the future. To be too affectionate would be dangerous, for too much love could ruin them. The parents seem to think that affection and tenderness should be carefully measured out in the child's best interest. And so the poor well-raised mother feels a duty toward her living children to train them well and to suppress their true feelings. But it's a different matter in the case of her dead child, for that child needs nothing from her and does not awaken any feelings of inferiority or hatred, does not cause her any conflict, does not offend her. Since she need not be afraid of spoiling the child with her love, when she goes to the cemetery she feels genuine inner freedom in her grief. Compared with that feeling, being with her other children can make her suffer because they clearly do not measure up to the dead child and its fantasized goodness and wisdom. Their vitality, their demands and claims on her can make a mother in love with her dead child feel distinctly insecure. They can cause feelings of helplessness and despair if she sees her pedagogical principles called into question.

This does not mean that the mother consciously wishes her children dead. Quite the contrary, she is even anxiously concerned that nothing happen to them; she paints them a picture of the constant danger threatening them, and she is apparently right about the danger, for something terrible has already happened. She must always keep an eye on her children, plaguing them with her close supervision and restricting their freedom. As a result, she has long since unavoidably forfeited her own vitality and spontaneity and in her depressed state is ultimately serving death.

We can imagine such a fate as this in the case of Käthe Kollwitz's mother. But how did the situation look from the child's perspective? Her mother's concern for her children's physical survival was a constant accompaniment for Käthe at play. In her memoirs Kollwitz mentions a pit that would make one blind if one fell into it, a sign that she took her mother's warnings to heart. She was also always attempting to satisfy her parents' pedagogical desires and become a quiet, well-behaved, uncritical, psychically dead little girl. Even if there are no dead siblings involved, such an attempt to suppress a child's spontaneity

Käthe Kollwitz, A Woman Entrusts Herself to Death
VAGA New York 1989

will intensify the child's depressive tendencies, because depression is an indication of the loss of vitality. When, however, as in the case of Käthe Kollwitz, three dead siblings are held up as model children, serving as proof of the mother's supposed capacity for love, then the daughter will do everything in her power—will readily sacrifice all her own feelings—to show herself truly "worthy" of her mother's love. Thus, psychic death, whose price is depression, gains double significance: it brings promise of the mother's unconditional, unlimited love, which the daughter has observed but has not experienced herself, and it satisfies the longing for death on the part of the mother, whose face looks transfigured, soft, almost happy only when she is standing by her children's graves.

I had reached this point in my thinking when I returned to the Kunsthaus in Zurich to see the exhibit of Kollwitz's graphic art. Now I felt that I had found my entirely personal—purely subjective, if you will—key to these pictures. For what had previously seemed rigid and difficult to empathize with now had gained life and meaning. And my hypotheses, based on the autobiographical material I had read, were fully confirmed by the pictures I saw.

In one picture a mother is stretching out her hand to greet Death (of whom we see only the right hand). Two little children with terrified faces are clinging to her skirts; their expression is in striking contrast to their mother's. Her look and her handshake are calm and friendly in a conventional way, as if she had opened the door to find a

31

familiar face, a friend or neighbor and not Death, and were saying, "Good evening, Mr. Jones. Please come in."

The theme "Mother with Dead Child" keeps reappearing in different ways. At the same time, death is shown as redeemer (transforming the child from an object of censure into one of love), as comforter (which the grave was for the mother), and as lover. This is how the daughter must have pictured death, I thought, when she heard her mother speak of it and watched her face. Now it was also clear to me that the stooped and lifeless woman I kept seeing, in group depictions as well, is not Käthe Kollwitz but her mother, as seen by one of her still living children. I also began to comprehend why so much resignation and hopelessness emanates from the group scenes, which lack the feeling of genuine anger one would expect from their theme: as a very young child, Käthe Kollwitz was threatened with punishment if she showed anger. The dead child being mourned is actually angry little Käthe herself.

As an adult Kollwitz was aware of the injustice of oppression, imprisonment, and exploitation on all sides, but she did not permit herself to cry out, just as she was not permitted to cry out as a child. Her socialism was not a revolutionary step for her; her father, brother, and husband were all socialists. By being one herself, she was in no way rebelling against her family but was, rather, in harmony with it; she had also tried to be pious in the pious setting of her childhood. She never freed herself from this dependency on her family's values and expectations of her. Her pictures express the hopelessness and resignation of

Käthe Kollwitz, Sitting Woman
VAGA New York 1989

a person who was not permitted to articulate her strong feelings because they made those around her uncomfortable. And because anger is missing from her works, it is not the feeling of pain that speaks in them but depression. The oversized figure of the mother mourning over Peter's grave also shows the familiar bent-over, depressed stance, but no pain. The father in Käthe Kollwitz's pictures hardly ever expresses anything but self-control.

Since I had now answered my questions in my own way, I no longer felt the need to track down all the details of this artist's life. I was about to return her diary to the library, having read only the sections about her childhood, when my eye was caught by a passage that confirmed my conjectures. Reminiscing about her mother, she writes:

> She often speaks of her first baby, who died a year after he was born. . . . The death of her first child must have been the most powerful experience in her life; that is why it is still so present for her now after fifty-five years.

And a little later she puts it even more plainly:

> Her awareness that her own child is now dead is blurred. She looks at the pictures of her babies, speaks in a tender voice of her "babies," and her eyes grow moist when she speaks of the first one who died. That happened nearly sixty years ago, but she still can't speak of him without being moved—and Julie dies and she grasps it only momentarily.

Her mother's eyes grow moist when she thinks of her child who died so long ago. Another daughter has just died, but this fact scarcely penetrates her consciousness. In the shadow of such a mother Käthe Kollwitz lived and painted her pictures of the dead child, which posterity would like to interpret simply as the expression of her social conscience and political commitment.

Buster Keaton with his parents

3

BUSTER KEATON:

Laughter at a Child's Mistreatment and the Art of Self-Control

*B*uster Keaton, the famous comedian of the twenties and thirties, could make people burst out laughing at his antics without cracking a smile himself. I can remember being bothered by this discrepancy as a child, and I wasn't able to find his antics funny when I had to look at that sad face. Lately, I chanced upon his biography by Wolfram Tichy and found in it the explanation for my discomfort. When he was only three, Buster Keaton started appearing on the stage with his parents, who were vaudeville performers, and helped to make them famous by taking severe abuse in front of an audience without batting an eyelash. The audience would squeal with delight, and by the time the authorities would be ready to intervene because of the physical injuries the little boy sustained, the family would already be performing in another city. In his autobiography, *My Wonderful World of Slapstick*, Keaton describes his situation plainly enough, but he describes only the *facts*, whose significance remained hidden to him. That this was the case can be seen from the following passage:

> *My parents were my first bit of great luck.* I cannot recall one argument that they had about money or anything else during the years I was growing up. . . . And from the time I was ten both they and the other actors on the bill treated me not as a little boy, but as an adult and a full-fledged performer. [Italics mine]

Had Buster Keaton realized that his parents were exploiting him shamelessly and brutally injuring not only his body but also his emotional life, he surely wouldn't have made a career of entertaining other people when he didn't feel like laughing himself. Keaton, quoted in Tichy's biography, reveals how he became the person he did:

> A child born backstage gets makeup smeared on his face by his parents as soon as he can walk . . . sometimes only for fun, for their own pleasure, and sometimes to see if the child is ready for an audience. . . . My father dressed me up in funny clothes, similar to the kind he wore himself. So from the beginning I wore pants and shoes that were too big for me. They brought me onstage when I was three, at first for matinées. When I had just turned four, a theater owner said, "If you bring him on for the evening performance, I'll pay

you $10 more." . . . From then on, I was part of the show, for $10 a week. . . . The first time I got paid was in 1899.

I appeared . . . before many different kinds of commissions, and in some cities before the mayor. In two states it was the governor who looked me over to see if I were being injured by the work that I did on the stage. Sometimes I was barred from appearing, but as our engagements were short, we would soon be in another town where the laws might be less strict.

In most cities and states, the laws specifically prohibited a child under sixteen doing juggling, wire work or acrobatics of any kind. This afforded a loophole for me, as I was not an acrobat. I did nothing except submit to being knocked about. When I went outside the theater, they used to dress me in long trousers, derby hat and hand me a cane to carry. In this way they fooled some people into believing that I was a midget.

In this knockabout act, my father and I used to hit each other with brooms, occasioning for me strange flops and falls. *If I should chance to smile, the next hit would be a good deal harder*. All the parental correction I ever received was with an audience looking on. *I could not even whimper*.

When I grew older, I readily figured out for myself that I was not one of those comedians who could jest with an audience and laugh with it. My audience must laugh *at* me. [Italics mine.]

One of the first things I noticed was that *whenever I smiled* or let the audience suspect how much I was enjoying myself *they didn't seem to laugh as much as usual*.

I guess people just never do expect any human mop,

dishrag, beanbag, or football to be pleased by what is being done to him. [Italics mine]

> If something tickled me and I started to grin, the old man would hiss, "Face! Face!" That meant freeze the puss. The longer I held it, why, if we got a laugh the blank pan or the puzzled puss would double it. He kept after me, never let up, and *in a few years it was automatic* [italics mine]. Then when I'd step onstage or in front of a camera, I *couldn't* smile. Still can't.

In view of his unwavering idealization of his parents, surely no one can doubt that the scenes described by Buster Keaton himself really took place. Nobody could make up anything so horrifying, especially not someone who claims to have had an ideal childhood. Yet he completely missed the *significance* of these scenes for his whole later life and for his art. The biographer misses it too. After he has put the facts together, Tichy writes, "*It is certain that Keaton's parents loved their son no less than other parents love their children* and treated him the way they subjectively thought right for everyone's interests" [italics mine].

This same biographer tells about the numerous times the father inflicted severe physical injury on his son and then even talked about it boastfully, proud that the boy put up with such treatment without complaining.

In spite of remembering what happened to him, Buster Keaton undoubtedly repressed the trauma of being abused and degraded. That is why he had to repeat the trauma countless times without ever *feeling* it, for the early lesson that his feelings were forbidden and were to be ignored retained its hold on him.

I have observed young people in the cafés and bars of a small city who also must have learned this lesson. They stare dully into space, cigarette in hand, sipping a glass of something alcoholic if they can afford it, and biting their fingernails. Alcohol, cigarettes, nail biting—all serve the same purpose: to prevent feelings from coming to the surface at any cost; as children these people never learned to experience their feelings, to feel comfortable with them, to understand them. They fear feelings like the plague and yet can't live entirely without them; so they pretend to themselves that getting high on drugs in a disco can make up for all they have lost. But it doesn't work. Cheated of their feelings, they begin to steal, to destroy property, and to ignore the feelings and rights of others. They don't know that all this was once done to them: they were robbed of their soul, their feelings were destroyed, their rights disregarded. Others were using them, innocent victims, to compensate for the humiliation they had once suffered themselves. For there is no way for mistreated children to defend their rights.

Society shares their ignorance. It puts these young people in reform schools, where they can perfect their destructive behavior at the expense of others while continuing to destroy themselves. We often hear people say that vandalism is on the increase nowadays, that young people were not always as violent, inconsiderate, and brutal as they are today. It's hard to say whether this is indeed

Buster Keaton with his parents

the case, because now certain forms of state-organized brutality such as war have disappeared—at least in Europe. But if it is actually true that today's youth are becoming increasingly unstable, then I wonder if it might not have something to do with the advancing technology surrounding childbirth and the manipulation of babies through medication, which make it impossible for newborns to experience their feelings and to orient themselves in terms of those feelings. I see a direct connection between infants tranquilized with drugs who can find no better alternatives in later life, and the adolescents in the bars whom I have just described.

What are young people to do with feelings that have been totally repressed but are still strongly active in the unconscious if the whole society ignores these feelings or denies that they are caused by child abuse? The only legal way to act out rage openly and violently in peacetime is in disciplining one's children. Since this outlet is not available to young people who have no children, they must look for another one. Suicide, addiction, criminal behavior, terrorism, and participation in organizations that sexually exploit children all can provide this kind of outlet—unless, like Buster Keaton, one can find it in creativity. Although creativity permits survival and helps a person to live with psychic damage, it still conceals rather than reveals the truth. Thus, it cannot protect the person from being self-destructive. As later chapters will show, Friedrich Nietzsche needed his entire philosophy to shield himself from knowing and telling what really happened to him.

Similarly, Buster Keaton learned to be creative without being able to laugh spontaneously. Neither of them became murderers or ended in prison, but they paid a great price for their denial of the truth. In addition, they were unable to help society understand the roots of destructive behavior and change its attitude toward children.

Chaim Soutine, Motherhood
1990 ARS N.Y./SPADEM

Chaim Soutine, Landscape
1990 ARS N.Y./SPADEM

4

Despot or Artist?

*A*bout five years ago I went to an exhibit of Chaim Soutine's paintings. I had felt very drawn to this painter for some time and had always had the impression that the great intensity of his work undeniably had its roots in childhood pain. The exhibit confirmed my impression and also provided me with important information. Along with the many portraits on display were numerous landscapes, which at first I didn't even look at because it was primarily the people—the strange, twisted, tormented figures—that fascinated me so. But when I did turn to the houses, streets, and squares, it struck me that they looked as though they might start to quiver at any moment.

I learned from the catalogue that Soutine was a Rus-

sian Jew who died in Paris in 1943. I asked myself whether
the extremely threatening situation of the Nazi Holocaust
had motivated, or even compelled, Soutine to paint the
world as shaking and falling apart. Then I thought of Kafka
and the discovery I had made in his case that visions of
the future have to do with one's earliest experiences and
that the repressed suffering of childhood can lend intensity
and expressiveness to an artist's work without his even
realizing what he is portraying. I wondered what it must
be like for a little child who is being beaten, lying across
someone's knee, head down so that the world looks upside
down. And this upside-down world is quivering, for his
body is shaken with every blow. That is how I experienced
Soutine's paintings even before I learned from the catalogue that he was frequently beaten by his parents and
brothers and could count on being punished regularly because he liked to draw so much, something that was forbidden by Orthodox Jews. The biographer who presented
these facts did not attribute any significance to them; he
defended the thesis that Soutine had a "narcissistic and
necrophilic character" and therefore loved to portray death.
The following passage, quoted from *Soutine* by Andrew
Forge, appeared in the catalogue:

> Smilovitchi, the Lithuanian village where [Soutine]
> was born [in 1893] the tenth son of the village tailor, was
> absolutely without culture. The very thought of painting
> pictures was heretical in such an orthodox community, and
> from the first Soutine was made to know that he was sin-

Adolf Hitler, A Church in Flanders
Archiv für Kunst und Geschichte, Berlin

ning: "Thou shalt not make unto thee any graven image or any likeness of anything that is in heaven above or that is in earth beneath or that is in the water under the earth." His struggle to find ways of breaking the Second Commandment is part of his legend: he stole from the household to buy a coloured pencil and was locked up in the cellar as punishment; he made a drawing of the village idiot, then asked the rabbi to pose for him. The aftermath reads like a parable: the rabbi's son beat him up severely, the rabbi paid Soutine's mother damages and with the money he was able to leave Smilovitchi to study at art school.

These details about Soutine's childhood traumas brought me back to the old question of why all battered children don't turn into monsters like Adolf Hitler, why some grow up to be brutal, unfeeling criminals and others highly sensitive people such as painters and poets who are capable of expressing their suffering. I detected the presence in Soutine's life history of a sympathetic and helpful witness who confirmed the child's perceptions, thus making it possible for him to recognize that he had been wronged.

Men of various professions frequently ask me why they didn't become a Hitler but have lived their lives as more or less peaceful physicians, lawyers, or professors, even though they, like Hitler, were beaten every day when they were children. They use this question to argue against my thesis that brutal, unfeeling, and thoroughly destructive treatment of children produces monsters—not by chance but of necessity. Then I always inquire about the details of the person's childhood, and on closer examination it turns out in *every* case that a particular witness helped the child experience his feelings to some degree. In Adolf Hitler's childhood, such a stabilizing witness was totally lacking. I have often compared the structure of Hitler's family to a totalitarian regime in which there is no possibility of recourse against the police state.

Hitler's father's arbitrary exercise of power was the highest authority, from which there was no escape. In the Third Reich, Adolf Hitler demonstrated the extent to which he had internalized this system. Not a single feeling or humane consideration existed that might have set limits to his cruelty once *he* achieved sole power. His use of power paralleled exactly the way he had been brought up. Whatever course of action his parents thought appropriate was carried out mercilessly with every measure of force possible. The boy was never permitted to doubt the rightness of his parents' decisions, for that would have resulted in unbearable torture. It was just as impossible for ordinary citizens in the Third Reich to question a decision made by the state or the Gestapo. If they tried, torture and death were the inevitable response. Brute force represented the ultimate power, and it provided its own "justification" for "maintaining order" and for the "legality" of its crimes; this practice, too, was borrowed from the structure of Hitler's family, in which everything—the stifling of feelings and creativity as well as the suppression of all the child's needs, indeed of almost every human emotion—was done in the name of a good upbringing.

Hitler's frenzied campaign against "degenerate art" also reflected what had been done to him: because colors awaken feelings in people, Hitler had to forbid them. Colors were dangerous, reprehensible, almost Jewish. So were vague lines, which excite the imagination. All signs of vitality had to be stamped out with the same thoroughness with which the child's vitality had been crushed by his parents for the sake of establishing order. Since order established by violent means was the highest value in this system, the annihilation of creativity was the obvious result. A student has investigated in detail the similarities between Hitler's upbringing and the concept of "degenerate art." Drawing on my writing and using pictures, including some done by Hitler, she presents convincing evidence that Hitler's attack on modern art was a continuation of the destructive process begun by his parents.

The Holocaust, the euthanasia law, and the concept of degenerate art are only a few examples of the way an adult perpetuates the destructive treatment he endured as a child. Hitler's aides accepted his methods without hesitation because for them too this system of coercion and enforced obedience had always been the only right one; they were comfortable with it and never questioned it. To combat cruelty, a person must first be able to perceive it as such. When someone has been exposed throughout childhood to nothing but harshness, coldness, coercion, and the rigid wielding of power, as Hitler and his closest followers were, when any sign of softness, tenderness, creativity, or vitality is scorned, then the person against whom that violence is directed accepts it as perfectly justified. Children believe they deserve the blows they are given, idealize their persecutors, and later search out objects for projection, seeking relief by displacing their supposed guilt onto other individuals or even a whole people. And in this way they become guilty themselves.

An artist like Soutine couldn't possibly have come from as destructive a totalitarian home setting as Hitler. The very fact that the boy was given money as compensation for being beaten and that his mother handed the money over to him shows that, despite the primitive conditions, someone was there for him in his childhood who helped him develop a sense of justice. Thus he did not have to blame himself for his suffering, to say nothing of globally displacing his guilt onto others later in life. Thanks to the money he was given as atonement, Soutine was even able to fulfill his fervent desire to take drawing lessons and go on to become a painter.

But there must have been other differences between Chaim Soutine's and Adolf Hitler's childhoods. Although they were both battered children and were severely punished for wanting to become artists, it is inconceivable that a person like Adolf Hitler could have grown up in the family of a poor Jewish tailor in Lithuania. It is just as inconceivable that Soutine the painter could have developed his subtle sense of color and his ability to express suffering as the son of Alois Hitler in Braunau. The hostility toward life and the destructive power of the Hitler family are evident from the abundance of available documents. The force of their message has now been brought to a wide audience in a stage drama that draws on many examples to show how any pleasure Hitler took in playing, in having ideas, or in being inventive was nipped in the bud by his parents' rigid emphasis on obedience and strict training.

Soutine did not grow up in an emotional desert as Hitler did. His upbringing was less systematic and consistent, less focused on obedience, for Jewish fathers in Eastern Europe were not trained to be harsh and brutal. They were not forced, like German fathers, to suppress their soft, helpless side from childhood on. It was quite natural for them to kiss and caress little children, and this was never called "monkey love."

Thus, the children of Jewish fathers were more likely to be shown tenderness, which undoubtedly contributed toward reducing the harm done to them. Without such tenderness and affection, children are unable to experience a feeling of pleasure that shows them what life is and lets them know that vitality is worth fighting for. This is a different kind of pleasure from that derived, for example, by tormenting animals, a means by which an abused child can act out humiliation. Even if children aren't given a love that is selfless, responsible, and protective, nevertheless physical closeness, caresses, and affection can arouse feelings in them—feelings such as longing, pain, loneliness, anger, and outrage but also delight in nature, in their own body, in the bodies of others, and especially in life. To be sure, this delight can be clouded or impaired by the way adults exercise their power, but again the emotional climate and the behavior of other people to whom a child is attached can make a difference. The poet Paul Celan's life is a good example. I found the following passages about his childhood in the biography by Israel Chalfen:

> Paul's father maintained strict discipline at home. He was not a good-natured person; he placed high demands on his son, punished him, beat him often for every minor childish infraction. Leo was small of stature, about a head shorter than his wife. One had the impression that he was attempting to compensate for his unimpressive appearance and his financial failures by being tyrannical at home. But he didn't quarrel with his wife—he was very devoted to her! It was his son who bore the brunt of his iron rule. Paul was a very sensitive child and no doubt suffered greatly from his father's severity. . . .
>
> Little Paul learned at an early age to be obedient and to behave in a way that corresponded to his parents' idea of a "good upbringing." He had to be fastidious about personal cleanliness, had to eat everything that was set before him, and was not allowed to ask superfluous questions. When he nevertheless did contradict, rebel, or display childish defiance, his father rebuked him roundly or even beat him. If the "offense" seemed especially grave, he shut the boy in an empty closet and took the key. Fortunately, the closet had a window opening onto the rear courtyard so that the women in the family could release the bitterly crying boy from his prison as soon as his father left the house on business matters. Usually it was his mother who came to the rescue, sometimes one of his aunts. . . .
>
> Paul encountered limits to his freedom of movement everywhere: he wasn't allowed to open doors from one room to another, nor was he allowed to go ouside without being accompanied by an adult. This also prevented him from being by himself on the quiet street, Wassilkogasse, with

its chestnut trees. On rare occasions he was permitted to play with the daughter, almost the same age as he, of a music teacher who lived in the same building, but only in the backyard, where there were a few trees and some sparse grass. Between the piles of wood stored there for the winter, between fence and back door lay the paradise of the first three years of Paul's life. It is not by chance that one of Celan's boyhood poems begins with the line "The world lies on the other side of the chestnut trees."

Even though Paul Celan's father ruled tyrannically, taking out on his son his own insecurity, the father was very devoted to his wife, and this in itself set limits to his tyranny. Mother and aunts could come to Paul's aid and let him out of the closet when he was imprisoned. These were the witnesses who rescued him, who helped him to understand that along with cruelty, rigidity, and stupidity there can also be mercy and goodness and that he was not guilty and wicked but was even lovable, although his father hadn't noticed.

Because of the women who came to his rescue, the boy was able to integrate into his consciousness the injustice he experienced, the pain of being imprisoned and tormented, without completely repressing it. But since he was raised so strictly, he was not permitted to see that he was being persecuted and held back in life by his own father. He had to keep his father's image sacred and displace his feelings onto other people and situations. All poets do this; they have to. That is why all his life Paul Celan could never break away from the theme of the concentra-

Chaim Soutine, Landscape with Houses
1990 ARS N.Y./SPADEM

tion camps, which were a menacing backdrop to his young adulthood and in which his parents died. He wrote poems about imprisonment that, significantly, were much admired in the postwar period, a time of strong intellectual defense against feelings in literature and art. These poems helped Celan express the sufferings of others in a masterful, restrained, and detached language. Yet his own childhood suffering, which was emotionally inaccessible, remained hidden from him.

The reason for Celan's suicide in 1970 at age forty-nine is not to be found in his war experiences, which he shared with many other survivors. If a person no longer has any room for hope, the cause—which has been repressed—lies in the far distant past. With his suicide, Paul Celan concluded the destructive work begun by his father, who denied his son the simplest, most harmless pleasures, even if they would not have cost anything, out of sheer meanness and for no apparent reason. It is so easy to do this to children because they are defenseless and at the mercy of adult whims, for better or worse. It is difficult for parents who were wounded as children to resist the temptation to exercise their power. If they were not allowed to play freely as children, they will keep finding reasons to deprive their own children of this enjoyment, which is so crucial for development. Or they will pervert play by an overemphasis on achievement—in sports such as ice skating or in music lessons—and destroy the child's creativity by instilling a compulsion to excel.

Celan's experience as a child was that the weak have

no rights, but he was not allowed to *know* it about himself on the conscious level. Instead, he described in poetic language the situation of the camp inmate whose life is also impaired without any reasons having to be given. The guards are able to destroy the enjoyment and dignity of a defenseless person as a matter of course because they too have learned this lesson at such an early age. Thus, Celan's poetry *is* authentic, even though its highly personal dimension remained hidden from the poet himself and from most readers. If he had understood the source of his suffering, he would have found meaning in life and might have enjoyed it.

It helped Celan to articulate his suffering by displacing the experience of his childhood onto the situation of the camp inmate, but it did not save him from suicide. If his father had not been murdered in a camp in 1942, Paul Celan might have found his way to the feelings of his childhood; perhaps he could have confronted his father inwardly and thereby saved his own life. But a person whose father has been cruelly murdered will find it very difficult to call him into question, even if for the sake of clarifying their relationship. It is easier to search for a way out in mysticism, whereby the person can close his eyes and conceal the truth in eloquent symbolic images. Yet sometimes this approach becomes virtually intolerable too because the power of the quite prosaic truth, the truth of the "little self" so disdained by the mystics, can be inexorable. Particularly for people who at some point in their childhood experienced loving care, this truth won't allow itself to be silenced completely, even with the help of poetry, philosophy, or mystical experiences. It insists on being heard, like every child whose voice has not been completely destroyed.

The absence or presence of a helping witness in childhood determines whether a mistreated child will become a despot who turns his repressed feelings of helplessness against others or an artist who can tell about his or her suffering. I could cite an abundance of further examples, but I will mention only a few. I must leave it to the reader to verify my statements, to supplement my evidence with new material, or to refute my arguments, as the case may be.

It's a fact that Dostoyevsky's father forced his children to read the Bible and tormented them with his greed. I don't know whether he mistreated them physically, and I must base my assumptions on my knowledge of his son's novels. But we do know that after his wife's death, he "led the life of a wastrel, drunkard, and tyrant. He treated his serfs with such cruelty that in 1839 they murdered him most brutally."

In mid-nineteenth-century Russia, cruelty toward serfs was almost the rule. The elder Dostoyevsky must therefore have treated his serfs especially brutally or perfidiously to drive them to such a dangerous act of revenge. How was this father likely to have treated his own sons? Perhaps a good deal could be gleaned from *The Brothers Karamazov*. But this novel also shows how difficult it is for sons to acknowledge a father's wickedness without feeling

Chaim Soutine, Landscape Cagnes
1990 ARS N.Y./SPADEM

guilty and without punishing themselves. The serfs were able to free themselves from the domination of their master, but the children were not. Fyodor Dostoyevsky suffered from epilepsy; he searched for God, Whom he could not find. Why didn't he become a criminal filled with hatred? Because he found a loving person in his mother. Because of her he experienced love, and this was crucial for his later life. Can the explanation be that simple? Yes. But the way his life turned out hung by a thread; it could easily have been completely different.

In contrast, as a child Stalin never experienced a protective and unpossessive love. Descriptions of his childhood do not reveal anyone in his life who protected him from the excessive beatings his father gave him or compensated for them with love and a watchful presence. His mother, who was very religious, is portrayed as confused and self-absorbed.

The family of Joseph Vissarionovich Djugashvili was unhappy in its own special way. The boy's father was a drunkard, a spendthrift, a man who possessed a violent temper, with no feeling for his wife or his son; he beat them unmercifully. He was a cobbler by trade, with a small shop in an obscure steet on the outskirts of Gori. The boy's mother was a quiet, withdrawn, deeply religious woman, beautiful in her youth, who found her chief pleasure in attending church services and in contributing out of her sparse earnings to the upkeep of the priests. She earned money by performing menial tasks in the houses of the rich, laundering, baking bread and running errands. She was also an occasional seamstress, and one of the boy's childhood friends, who was not unsympathetic to him, remembered that she sometimes earned a living by cutting, sewing and laundering underwear. She was a proud woman and kept her sufferings to herself.

When Ekaterina Geladze married Vissarion Djugashvili in 1874, she was a girl of seventeen and her husband was twenty-two. The first three children are said to have died in childbirth, Joseph, born on December 21, 1879, being the only child to grow to maturity. Vissarion died when the boy was in his eleventh year, and Ekaterina survived her husband by nearly fifty years. She was a small, fragile, indomitable woman, who remained deeply religious throughout her life and always wore a black nunlike costume.

The family of Stalin might have come out of Gorky's play *The Lower Depths*. It was brutally unhappy. They lived in grinding poverty, constantly in debt. Sometimes the neighbors would have pity on the struggling seamstress and her undernourished son; and their pity may have done more harm to Joseph than the beatings he received from his father. Sometimes poverty drove Ekaterina close to madness, and we hear of her wandering through the streets with her hair disheveled, crying, praying, singing and muttering to herself. From a very early age the boy knew what it was to live alone in the world.

According to Iremashvili, who knew the family well and was constantly in and out of the house, the father beat the son vengefully, remorselessly, with a kind of brooding, deliberate passion, without pleasure and without any sense of guilt or wrongdoing, for no other purpose than to provide himself with some excitement in an otherwise empty and purposeless existence. The result was inevitable. The boy learned to hate. Most of all he hated his father, but gradually this hatred expanded until it included all other fathers, all other men.

"I never saw him crying," Iremashvili relates, and the statement has the ring of authenticity. The boy became hardened by his beatings, and became in the end terrifyingly indifferent to cruelty. His face and body were covered with bruises, but he was determined not to surrender. Somehow he would survive his father, but in order to survive it was necessary to become as brutal as his father. He was too puny to hit back, but he could provide himself with a brutal protective armor of indifference and scorn. "Those undeserved and fearful beatings," says Iremashvili, "made the boy as hard and heartless as his father." . . .

Church was a consolation, for no one beat him in church, no one scorned him or had pity on him. As a choirboy he walked in processions, sang hymns, wore brilliant vestments, and being close to the priests, he was closer to the source of the mystery. His earliest ambition was to be a priest; and his mother looked forward to the time when she would be blessed by her son.

His greatest consolation however was his mother, who worked herself to the bone to provide for him and who lived for him. . . . Her love for her son was an intense and possessive love. . . .

(It is obviously still possible for most biographers to designate as love both destructive attempts to possess one's child and total blindness to the child's situation.)

He was seven when he suffered an attack of smallpox, which left disfiguring scars that remained to the end of his life. It must have been a serious attack, for the scars were large and numerous, with the result that when he came to power thousands of photographs of him had to be carefully doctored.

An even more distressing affliction occurred when he was about ten. He only once spoke about it, and then only briefly when he was explaining why, when he was in exile in Siberia during World War I, he was not called up for military service. He told the story to Anna Alliluieva, his sister-in-law, who published it in her memoirs:

> The left arm of Stalin was badly bent at the elbow. The injury occurred during his childhood. An infection set in, and since there was no one to give it treatment, blood-poisoning followed. Stalin was close to death.
>
> "I don't know what saved me," he told us. "Either it was due to my healthy organism or to the ointments smeared on it by the village quack, but I got my health back again."
>
> The vestiges of that injury remain to the present day. . . .

As a result of the injury Stalin's left arm was some three inches shorter than the right, and he never had complete muscular control of his left hand. At various times he wore a brace to support the elbow; the outline of the brace can be seen in several photographs. A distinguished orthopedic surgeon has suggested on the basis of Alliluieva's account and a number of photographs that Stalin suffered "a compound fracture with resultant osteomyelitis and a subsequent hand deformity secondary to disturbance of growth of the arm, the hand deformity being produced by a Volkman's contracture subsequent to improper treatment of the fracture."

Such a diagnosis is, of course, largely speculative.

Chaim Soutine, Portrait of a Child
1990 ARS N.Y./SPADEM

The medical records of Stalin have never been published, and it is unlikely that they will be published for some years to come. What is certain is that the left arm was warped, lacked the strength of the right arm, and caused him pain and discomfort throughout his life. The awkward shoulder brace was a constant reminder that he suffered from an incurable deformity, and he had only to look at his left hand, which never opened properly, to remember that he was not like other men. He went to considerable trouble to conceal his deformity, which could only be successfully hidden when he was wearing a heavy greatcoat with unusually long sleeves. The crooked arm probably had a profound effect on his emerging character.

There is no clue as to how the injury occurred. It seems likely to have happened as a result of one of the ferocious beatings he received from his father.

Untreated fractures of the left arm are a frequently occurring phenomenon in battered children. The adult holds in his right hand the broomstick or clothes hanger used in a frontal attack on the child standing before him, and the child's left arm is exposed to the greatest danger.

Stalin's family was very poor, and his mother had to work. But Charlie Chaplin's mother was poor too. She even had to put her child in an orphanage, but she visited him there and gave him the assurance that he was loved, that he was valuable and important to someone. The experience of being loved can be sensed in all the Chaplin films. In spite of hunger, misery, and calamity, there is always room for feelings, for tears, for tenderness, for life.

For Stalin—who, like Hitler, was born after the death of several siblings—there was nothing but loneliness, the constant threat of beatings, the belief in his own ostensible worthlessness and guilt, and nowhere another human being to protect him from constant persecution and abuse, to tell or show him that he was not guilty. There was no one of influence in his life who could avert his fate, just as there was no mercy later for the millions of prisoners in the Gulag Archipelago. Without even being sentenced, they could be tormented, tortured, killed—or released— for no apparent cause. Everything was determined by the arbitrary whim of a tyrant who suspected enemy attacks from all sides because he had experienced perpetual threats at an early age and because there had been no witness to teach him that the whole world was not like his father: wicked, dangerous, unpredictable, frightening. When a child's boundless powerlessness never finds sheltering arms, it will be transformed into harshness and merci- lessness; when, in addition, it is spurred by a mother's ambition, it can result in a great career that introduces all the elements of the child's repressed misery into world history. Then millions of human beings are marched to Russian prisons or to Nazi gas chambers without knowing why, because once a little boy didn't know why he was being punished. How long are we going to tolerate these senseless marches now that we finally are in a position to discover their underlying causes?

Friedrich Nietzsche, 1861
Ullstein Bilderdienst

TWO

Friedrich Nietzsche:
The Struggle Against the Truth

A Mistreated Child, a Brilliant Mind, and Eleven Years of Darkness

*S*everal years ago I wanted to demonstrate that the works of writers, poets, and painters tell the encoded story of childhood traumas no longer consciously remembered in adulthood. After having made this discovery in my own painting and in the writings of Franz Kafka, I was able to test it against other life histories. I wanted to share what I had found with biographers and psychoanalysts, but I soon learned that I was dealing with forbidden knowledge, by no means easy to share with "the experts."

And so I decided not to publish my study but to keep the knowledge I had gained to myself, devoting myself to other pursuits such as painting and confronting my own early childhood. Through these activities I gradually realized that my disappointment at the blindness of society and of the experts had something to do with my own blindness and that I really felt compelled to try to prove something to myself that a part of me refused to believe. Of course, I had long been aware of my parents' weaknesses, of the injury they had inflicted on me without knowing it, but my early idealization of my parents was still unresolved. I recognized it in my naive belief and confidence that the biographers of Hitler, Kafka, and Nietzsche must be capable of seeing and affirming what I had found.

That they were not capable of recognizing such forbidden knowledge finally became clear to me when I realized how strongly I was clinging to my childhood idealization of my parents. For a long time I couldn't stop hoping that my parents would someday be ready to share my questions with me, to stop evading them, react to them, and not be afraid to join me in seeing where they led. This never happened when I was a child, and I thought I had long since gotten over my deprivation. But my astonishment at the reactions of people whom I had expected to be more knowledgeable than I revealed that I still had not given up the image of clever and courageous parents who could be convinced by the facts. Once I became conscious of the connection, I no longer had any need to publish my study.

Now I have a different motivation for publishing. I would like to share the knowledge I have gained with people who can face the facts. They need not be experts but, rather, people who may be inspired by my work to read Nietzsche and to make a connection between their impressions of him and their own experience.

The need to share my findings with others was not my only motive in writing about Nietzsche. My work with the Nietzsche material had made me realize that society's ignorance about the injuries inflicted on children represents a great danger for humanity. Sentences from Nietzsche's writings could never have been misinterpreted in support of fascism and the annihilation of human beings if people had understood his words for what they were: the encoded language of the child who was forbidden to express his true feelings. Young men would never have been willing to march to war with his words in their pack if they had known that his ideology promoting the destruction of morality and traditional values such as charity and mercy stood for the raised fist of a child starved for truth who had suffered severely under the domination of hypocrisy. Since I myself had witnessed the way the deadly marching of the National Socialists in the thirties and forties was indirectly spurred on by Nietzsche's words, it now seemed to me worth the trouble to find and call attention to the genesis of these words, thoughts, and feelings.

Would Nietzsche's ideas have been useless to the Nazis if people had understood their source? I do not doubt it. But if society *had* understood, then the ideas of the Nazis would also have been unthinkable or at least would not have found the broad acceptance they did. The simple, commonplace facts of child abuse are not given a hearing; if they were, the human race would have greater understanding and wars could be prevented. Only if they are presented in a disguised, symbolic form can they arouse great interest and an emotional response. For the disguised story is, after all, familiar to most of us, but its symbolic language must guarantee that what has been repressed will not be brought to light and cause pain. Therefore, my thesis that Nietzsche's works reflect the unlived feelings, needs, and tragedy of his childhood will probably meet with great resistance. The thesis is correct nevertheless, and I will offer proof in the pages that follow. My proof can be understood, however, only by someone who is willing to temporarily abandon the adult perspective to gain insight into and take serious account of the situation of a child.

Which child are we talking about? The boy who learns in school to suppress his normal, human feelings and always act as if he didn't have any? The little boy who is trained day after day by his young mother, his grandmother, and his two aunts to be a "strong" man? The very little boy whose beloved father "loses his mind" and goes on living with the family for eleven months in an unstable condition? Or the even younger child who was punished most severely and locked in dark closets by the father whom he loved and was occasionally allowed to play with? It is not one or another but all these children rolled into one who had to bear so much without being allowed to express any feelings or, indeed, even to have any feelings. He was not supposed to cry, to scream, to be in a rage. He was only supposed to be well disciplined and to do brilliant work.

Friedrich Nietzsche survived this childhood; he survived the more than one hundred illnesses in one year of secondary school, the constant headaches, and the rheumatic ailments, which his biographers have assiduously listed without searching for their cause and which they finally attribute to a "weak constitution." At the age of twelve he kept a diary, the kind an adult might have kept, written in a well-adjusted, reasonable, well-behaved way. But in adolescence his once suppressed feelings burst forth, resulting in works that would deeply move other young people of later generations. And then at age forty, when he could no longer bear his loneliness and, since he was not able to see that the roots of his life history went back to his childhood, he lost his mind and everything became "clear": historians locate the cause of his tragic ending in a venereal disease he supposedly contracted as an adolescent. The outcome is in keeping with our moral standards: the just, though delayed, punishment, in the form of a fatal disease, for having visited a prostitute. This is similar to the present attitude toward AIDS. Everything seems to turn out for the best, and hypocritical morality is restored. But what those who raised and taught Nietzsche actually did to the boy did not happen so long ago that we can no longer find out about it. Young graduate students can uncover the story, read the letters from his sister and others, write dissertations about their findings, and reconstruct the situation that gave rise to his later works, such as *Beyond Good and Evil, The Antichrist,* and *Thus Spake Zarathustra.* But this can be done only by students who were not mistreated as children or who have worked through their mistreatment and therefore have open ears and eyes for the suffering of battered children. Their research is not likely to be greeted with enthusiasm by their professors. If they can persevere in their research nonetheless, they will produce evidence that the crimes committed against children have serious effects on all humanity. They will also be able to illustrate the unexpected ways in which these effects occur.

FAMILY LIFE

In my search for the facts about Nietzsche's early childhood I learned the following:

Both parents were the children of Protestant ministers and numbered several theologians among their forebears. Nietzsche's father was the youngest child from his own father's second marriage; when, at age thirty, he married a seventeen-year-old woman, he also took in both of his older, unmarried sisters and, later, his mother. Friedrich was born a year after the marriage, in 1844. When Friedrich was two, his sister was born and soon after that a brother, who died at the age of two shortly after the death of the father. According to reports, the father was a warmhearted and feeling person who from the first loved his son very much and frequently had him by his side when he improvised at the piano. This important experience and the warmth the father may have shown his son probably played a role in enabling the boy to experience strong feelings in spite of his rigorous upbringing. Despite his affection, however, the father strictly forbade certain feelings and severely punished his son for expressing them. There are reports of temper tantrums, which stern measures soon put to an end.

His father, when he had time, liked to spend it with his oldest child, once the boy had learned to talk a little. It didn't disturb him either when Friedrich came into the father's study and watched him "quietly and thoughtfully," as the mother writes, while he was working. But the child was completely spellbound when his father sat at the piano and "improvised." Already at the age of one, little Fritz, as everyone called him, would then sit up in his carriage, listen, quiet as a mouse, and not take his eyes off his father. Otherwise, however, he was not always a well-behaved child in those first years. If he didn't get his way, he threw himself to the floor and furiously kicked his little legs in the air. His father must have taken very energetic measures against this behavior, yet for a long time the boy was still stubborn and recalcitrant when he was denied something he wanted, although he no longer rebelled but withdrew silently into a quiet corner or to the privy, where he vented his anger by himself.

Whatever a biographer may mean by "venting" here, the feelings that had to be eliminated in the privy are unmistakably present in the philosopher's later writings. We mustn't forget that a grandmother and two young aunts also lived with the family. In addition to their charitable activities and their help with the household, they were mainly concerned with the upbringing of the firstborn child. When Friedrich was scarcely four, his father died after eleven months of suffering from a serious illness, probably the result of a brain tumor, which his son later referred to as "softening of the brain." The family perpetuated the story that the father's illness was caused by an accident, a version of events that somewhat lessened the shame that a brain disease may have caused them. The actual medical diagnosis is not completely clear to this day.

It is difficult for us as adults to imagine how a child of four feels when his beloved father, his closest attachment figure (which his mother at that time was not), suddenly becomes ill with a brain disease. At the very least Nietzsche must have been highly perplexed. His father's previously more or less predictable reactions were so no longer; the great, admired, and clever man had suddenly become "stupid." His family was perhaps embarrassed at the answers he gave to questions. Possibly the boy too was scornful, but he had to suppress his scorn because he loved his father. We can assume that this same father, who disappeared so soon as his son's companion, was proud of the child's intelligence. But as the father's illness progressed, the boy could no longer tell him things or ask him questions, no longer use him as a point of orientation or count on his response. Yet despite his condition, the father was still present.

Soon after the death of his father, Nietzsche's little brother died too, and now Friedrich was left as the only male in a household of women—his grandmother, two aunts, mother, and younger sister. This might have turned out well for him if one of these women had treated him with tenderness, warmth, and genuine concern. But they all tried to outdo one another in teaching him self-control and other Christian virtues. The originality of his imagination and the honesty of his questions were too much for their sense of morality, and so they attempted to silence the child's curiosity, which made them uncomfortable, by strict supervision and a stern upbringing.

What else can a child, so completely at the mercy of a regimen like this, do except adapt and suppress his genuine feelings with all his might? That is what Friedrich did, and he soon became a model child and a model pupil. One biographer describes a scene that clearly illustrates how extreme the boy's self-denial was. Caught in heavy rain on his way home from school, Nietzsche did not quicken his pace but continued to walk slowly with head erect. His explanation was that "upon leaving school one must go home in a calm and mannerly way. That's what the regulations require." We can imagine the training that must have preceded such behavior.

The boy observed the people around him and could not help but be critical; however, he was forced to keep such thoughts to himself and do all he could to suppress them, along with any other impious thoughts. In addition, he constantly heard the Christian virtues of neighborly love and compassion being preached all around him. Yet in his own daily experience no one took pity on him when he was beaten; no one saw that he was suffering. No one came to his aid, even though so many people around him were busy practicing the Christian virtues. What good are these virtues, the little boy must have kept asking himself. Am I not also the "neighbor" who deserves to be loved? But even questions such as these could have provoked more beatings. What choice did he have, then, but to keep his questions to himself and to feel even more alone with them than before because he could not share them with anyone?

But the questions did not go away. Later, much later, after Nietzsche finished his schooling and had nothing to fear from the authorities—in this case his professors—because he had become a professor himself, the questions and repressed feelings broke out of the prison where they had been locked up for twenty years. In the meantime, by finding an ersatz object they gained social legitimacy. Nietzsche did not direct his criticism at the real causes of his rage—his aunts, his grandmother, his mother—but at the values of his chosen field, philology. Still, this took courage, for they were values that had until then been held sacred by *all* philologists.

But Nietzsche also attacked values that once were dear to him although not respected by those around him —for example, the "truth," symbolized in the person of Socrates. In the same way that a person going through puberty must first reject everything he once loved in order to establish new values for himself, Nietzsche—who never revolted during puberty, who at the age of twelve made agreeable entries in his diary—now at twenty-five set out to attack the culture he had grown up with, to mock it, to make it seem absurd by standing it on its head. He did this not with the methods of a growing adolescent but with the highly developed intellect of a philologist and professor of philosophy.

It is all too understandable that his language became forceful and impressive. It was not empty talk that seized upon trite revolutionary slogans but a combination of original thoughts and intense feelings, rarely found in a philologist, that had a direct impact on the reader.

We are accustomed to thinking of Nietzsche as a representative of late Romanticism and to seeing the influence of Schopenhauer on his work. Which people influence us as adults is no accident, and Nietzsche's description of the euphoria he felt when he opened Schopenhauer's major opus, *The World as Will and Idea* (1819), and began reading indicates that he had good reason for discovering in Schopenhauer a world intimately related to his own. If he had been allowed to speak freely in his family as an adolescent, it is possible that he would not have needed Schopenhauer or, above all, the Germanic heroes, Richard Wagner, and the concept of the "blond beast." He would have found his own discriminating words with which to say: "I can't bear the chains that shackle me day after day; my creative powers are in danger of being destroyed. I need all my energies to rescue them and to assert myself in your midst. There is nothing I can confront you with that you would understand. I can't live in this narrow, untruthful world. And yet I can't leave you. I can't get along without you because I'm still a child and am dependent on you. That's why you have so much power although you are essentially weak. It takes heroic courage, superhuman qualities, and super-human strength to crush this world that is interfering with my life. I don't have that much strength; I am too weak and afraid of hurting you, but I despise the weakness in me and the weakness in you, which forces me to pity you. *I despise every form of weakness* that interferes with my life. You have surrounded me with restrictions; prisoner that I am of school and home, there is no free space for me except perhaps in music, but that is not enough for me. I must be able to use words. I must be able to shout them out. Your morality and your reason are a prison for me in which I am smothering to death, and this at the beginning of my life when I would have so much to say."

Words such as those got stuck in Nietzsche's throat and brain, and it is no wonder that he suffered continually from severe headaches, sore throats, and rheumatic ail-ments as a child and especially during his school days. What he was not allowed to say out loud remained active in his body in the form of constant tension. Later he could direct his criticism against abstract concepts such as cul-ture, Christianity, philistinism, and middle-class values without having to worry that someone might die as a result (all well-brought-up children are afraid that their angry words might kill those they love). Compared with this danger, criticism of society in the abstract is harmless for an adult, even if society's representatives are outraged by it. An adult is not facing them like a helpless, guilty child; an adult can use intellectual arguments to defend himself and even to make attacks—methods not usually available to a child and not available to Nietzsche as a child.

And yet Nietzsche's accurate observations concerning Western culture and Christian morality as well as the vehement indignation they aroused in him do not date from the period of his philosophical analysis but from his first years of life. It was then that he perceived the system and suffered under it, simultaneously as slave and devotee; it was then that he was chained to a morality he despised and was tormented by the people whose love he needed. Because of his brilliant intellect, the perceptions he stored up at an early age have helped many people see things they have never seen before. The experiences of one individual, despite their subjectivity, can have universal validity because the family and the child-rearing methods minutely observed at an early age represent society as a whole.

PUZZLEMENT

Along with its positive side, however, Nietzsche's manner of "mastering" his fate as a child had a devastating and disastrous effect because he used what had caused him the most trouble—his puzzlement—as a weapon against the world. In the same way that *he* became thoroughly puzzled—first by his father's terrible illness and later by the unbearable contradiction between the morality preached to him and the actual behavior of the attachment figures in his family and in school—he sometimes puzzles the reader, probably without knowing it. I had this feeling of puzzlement when I recently began reading Nietzsche again after three decades. Thirty years ago I would surely have disregarded my puzzlement because my only concern then was to understand his meaning. But now I let myself be guided by the feeling. As a result, I realized that other readers must have felt the same way, even if they did not use the word *puzzlement* and attributed their feelings to their own lack of education, intelligence, or depth. Blaming ourselves is exactly the reaction we learn as children. If the grown-ups (who are supposed to be more clever than we are) self-assuredly assert things that are inconsistent, contradictory, or absurd, how can children raised in an authoritarian way be expected to know that what they are hearing is not the ultimate wisdom? They will make every effort to accept it as such and will carefully conceal their doubts from themselves. This is the way many people read the writings of the great Nietzsche today. They blame themselves for their puzzlement and show Nietzsche the same reverence he must have shown his ill father as a child.

Although admitting my perplexity helped me recognize these connections, I do not consider my feeling to be simply a personal matter. I found a passage by Richard Blunck—who devoted himself to Nietzsche's life and work for forty years—that indirectly confirms my own impression. Since a large portion of the material Blunck had collected was destroyed in the war, he himself never published the major Nietzsche biography he had planned but left further work on it to Curt-Paul Janz. I found these words by Blunck in the introduction to Janz's first volume:

Friedrich Nietzsche and His Mother
Ullstein Bilderdienst

Those who come across a book of Nietzsche's for the first time, the way we did forty years ago, immediately sense that more is required to understand it than the intellect, that more is involved here than following someone's thinking from premise to conclusion and from concept to concept in order to arrive at "truth." They will feel that they have wandered instead into an immense field of force that is emitting shock waves of a far deeper nature than can be registered by intellect alone. They will be struck less by the opinions and insights expressed than by the person behind these opinions and insights. Readers will often react defensively to them if they have something to defend, but they will never again be entirely able to escape the man who expressed them. If readers pursue these ideas that confront, sometimes even assault, them in the form of commanding sentences, then they will soon have the feeling that they are in a labyrinth in whose intricate passageways they find not only immeasurable riches but also the threatening visage of a minotaur who demands human sacrifice. They will believe they are encountering the truest of truths, which go to the heart of things, only to have these truths cancel themselves out in the next book and to feel themselves thrust into a new passageway of the labyrinth. Still, if they have an alert mind and not merely a groping intellect, they will never lose the certainty that Nietzsche has brought them closer to life and its secrets than has any other thinker. Despite the contradictory character of his views and positions, a more profound and elevated intellectual force is communicated that is not confined to positions and truths but constantly both ignores and transcends them in the service of an authenticity that knows no law other than itself and the eternal flux of life with all its tranformations and creativity.

Such authenticity, however, does not consist in collecting knowledge and ordering things in a rational manner, little as it can do without these processes, but is a feature of the ethical personality, of the heart's courage, and the dauntless and indefatigable nature of the mind. It must be lived and suffered if it is to attain that intellectual force which Nietzsche's work demonstrates. And it is because his authenticity—in combination with a great receptivity to all aspects of the European intellectual tradition as well as a critical grasp of this tradition, in combination also with a profound understanding of human nature and a prophetic farsightedness and clarity of vision—is apparent to an extent unequalled in the history of Western thought that Nietzsche's life and work affect us so powerfully. Spurred on by this authenticity, he waged a single-minded, unwearying struggle against an age that was sinking deeper and deeper into hopeless dishonesty, a struggle against his own happiness, against fame, and even against his tender heart. This was an undertaking whose purity and necessity cannot be obscured or cancelled out, no matter how ambiguous or even dreadful its effects.

Because of his own upbringing, the author of these lines, who actually was very close to the truth, got caught in the labyrinth he refers to and was unable to track down its biographical origins; and if he *had* dared to do so, his life and work in the Third Reich would surely have been jeopardized. For Nietzsche was very much in vogue when Blunck was doing his work in pre–World War II Germany. His glorification of the "barbaric hero" was taken literally and was lived out with all its horrible consequences. But the very way the National Socialists adapted Nietzsche's ideas and formulations for their own purposes shows how dangerous it can be to view the last links in a biographical chain in isolation while remaining uninterested in and blind to the earliest links in the chain.

Today Nietzsche's biographers emphasize again and again a closer connection between his life and thought than biographers of other philosophers do. Yet Nietzsche's biographers rarely refer to his childhood, despite the fact that without understanding this crucial period a life remains an enigma. The two-thousand-page biography by Janz, which appeared in 1978, devotes less than ten pages to Nietzsche's childhood (not counting a genealogical history). Since the importance of childhood for later life is still a very controversial subject, biographers have done little investigation in this area. Nietzsche scholars search in his work for connections to the history of philosophy rather than to his life. His life, his illness, and his tragic ending, to say nothing of his work, have never been examined in the light of his childhood.

And yet today it seems to me a simple matter to recognize that what Nietzsche wrote was his hopeless attempt, which he didn't abandon until his breakdown, to free himself from his prison by expressing his unconscious but present hatred for those who raised and mistreated him. His hatred, and his fear of it, became all the more vehement the less he succeeded in becoming independent of its objects, his mother and sister. It is a known fact that his sister altered many of his letters for publication, that she intrigued untiringly to the detriment of his true interests and did not rest until his relationship with Lou Andreas Salomé was destroyed. Both mother and sister needed Friedrich's dependence on them until the very end. Since the perfectly raised child had learned at an early age not to defend himself but to struggle instead against his true feelings, the grown man was unable to find his way to real liberation. His writing kept alive the illusion of liberation because on a symbolic level he actually did take steps in the direction of truth and freedom. He took them in his life as well but only insofar as they did not involve the members of his family. After he became ill, for instance, he had the courage to give up his professorship in Basel to have more freedom to criticize the academic system. He was then free to write what he needed to say instead of having to conform to the demands of the university. But this was still an ersatz solution as long as he was unable to recognize his idealization of his parents, who were responsible for his suffering. For his true feelings (of anger, fear, contempt, helplessness, the wish to be free, destructive rage, and desperate dependence on his persecutors), originating in childhood, gave him no peace and kept demanding new ersatz objects.

HIS MOTHER

In several letters to Nietzsche's friends after the philosopher had completely lost his mental faculties, his mother describes the condition of the patient for whom she has sacrificed herself and whom she takes care of like a little child. In one letter she writes that her son uttered terrible screams although he had a cheerful expression on his face. We can't be sure how reliable this information is because mothers frequently interpret a look on a child's face in keeping with their own wishes. But if his mother's observation was correct, then the explanation may be that, in her presence, the very little child was allowed to scream loudly for the first time in his life and that he was enjoying the tolerance he had finally won from her. For we can scarcely conceive of someone screaming without a face racked with pain.

There are women who can be kinder to their children if the children are no longer capable of thinking (that is, of being critical), as the result of mental illness or a brain disease, for example. Although not yet dead, the children are helpless and totally dependent on the mother. If such a woman was brought up to fulfill her duty above all else, she will feel good and noble if she sacrifices herself for her child. If she had to suppress her own criticism as a child, it will make her angry the moment her son or daughter expresses criticism of her. She feels less threatened, on the other hand, by a handicapped child. In addition, her self-sacrifice is respected and admired by society. Thus, it is very likely that Nietzsche's mother—who was only eighteen when he was born and is described as cold, stupid, and disinterested even by sympathetic biographers—actually did sacrifice herself to look after her son in his last years when he no longer recognized his friends and could barely speak.

RICHARD WAGNER
(The Father: Seduction and Disappointment)

It would take a very careful reading of Nietzsche's letters to relate the individual episodes in his life to his childhood. In addition, the actual facts would have to be sifted from his sister's numerous falsifications. I can imagine that anyone who is not afraid of taking on the task of establishing the connections to his childhood would discover much that is new. One might look into the question, for instance, of whether Nietzsche's relationship with Richard Wagner, who was thirty years his senior, was not a repetition of the repressed tragic experience with his father, who had taken ill so suddenly. This conjecture seems justified by the fact that his initial admiration and enthusiasm for Wagner, beginning about 1868 and nurtured at Wagner's home in Bayreuth, so quickly turned into disappointment, rejection, and radical estrangement. Nietzsche's break with Wagner culminated in 1882 when Wagner wrote *Parsifal*, which in Nietzsche's eyes "betrayed" the old Germanic values for the sake of highly suspect Christian ones. Not until then did he become fully conscious of weaknesses in Richard Wagner, weaknesses he had previously overlooked in his idealization of the older man.

I have searched in vain in the extensive secondary literature about Nietzsche for information describing how the highly intelligent four-and-a-half-year-old child reacted to his father's fatal brain disease that lasted nearly a year. For lack of any indication in his youth, I turned to his later life and looked for clues there. I believe I found them in Nietzsche's relationship with Richard Wagner. However great the disappointment in Wagner's work may have been for the mature Nietzsche, it would never have provoked such an extreme degree of mockery and contempt (especially since Wagner hadn't done any- thing to alienate Nietzsche personally and was even very fond of him) if Wagner's personality and music hadn't reminded him of his father and of the misery of his early childhood.

From the mid-1870s, Wagner's entire work and the Bayreuth atmosphere, in which Nietzsche had previously felt at home, struck him as a gigantic lie. The one thing he could not deny was Wagner's dramatic gift, although he did not compliment Wagner with this admission, for he defined the psychology and morality of an actor in the following way: "One is an actor by virtue of being ahead of the rest of mankind in one insight: what is meant to have the effect of truth must not be true. . . . Wagner's music is never true. But *it is taken for true*; and thus it is in order." Wagner's music, according to Nietzsche, con- tained the pretense of sacred, noble, great, and good feel- ings, the hoax of pseudo ideals that have little to do with the authentic feelings of real people, such as Nietzsche found embodied in Bizet's *Carmen* (1875), with its ambiv- alence and its "killing for love." He saw *Carmen* several times with great enthusiasm, experiencing it as a liberation from the lie that had afflicted him not only since his younger years with Wagner in Bayreuth but even since his childhood. And now his attack against the fatherly friend he once admired, Richard Wagner, turned into a total one: he no longer saw anything good in him and hated him with all his heart like a deeply wounded child. His hatred was nourished by despair and grief over having let himself be deceived for so long, for admiring someone for so long whom he now considered contemptible. Why didn't he see through the weakness behind the facade sooner? How could he have been so mistaken?

Nietzsche saw himself as the victim of a seduction that he must now unmask by every means at his command. He found Wagner's admirers naive and could not grasp that they continued to go to Bayreuth, where they allowed themselves to be hypnotized by a lie, after he himself had seen through it. The pain this caused him kept showing through in the aspersions he cast on Wagner: Nietzsche would have liked to save the world from a great deception and bring the Wagnerians to their senses; he would have liked to lead them back to themselves and their own genuine experiences the way Zarathustra did by refusing to have any disciples.

Although Nietzsche's attacks derived their intensity from his repressed rage against his father and other attachment figures from childhood, they did not display any weakness in logic that would reveal their real roots. What he wrote about Wagner and substantiated with examples was so convincing (although probably not for Wagnerians) that it retains its claim to objectivity quite apart from the subjective, highly emotional background of his observations. I believe that Nietzsche's keen powers of observation had their beginnings in his relationship with his father, to whose music the little boy listened with rapt attention, admiration, and enthusiasm. But his father was not only a musician who played the piano but also a pedagogue who approved of certain feelings (such as his son's enthusiasm for his playing) but severely punished the display of others.

Perhaps the boy succeeded in accepting his father's two different sides and in overlooking the punishment as long as he was allowed to be with his father, to listen to his music making and let the music become part of him. But when his father fell ill and the child felt suddenly and completely abandoned by him, overwhelming feelings of disappointment, rage, and shame at being seduced and then forsaken would have had to break through—*if* the boy had not already learned that it was not permissible to show such feelings and if he had not been subsequently raised exclusively by women ("female Wagnerians") who condemned his feelings and kept them in the strictest rein. These feelings had to lie in wait for decades until they could be experienced toward another musician.

The sharpness and accuracy of Nietzsche's later observations about Wagner not only were unimpaired by his feelings but, on the contrary, seemed to be intensified by them. If it had not been made impossible for him to speak out, Nietzsche the child might have said: "I don't believe your music if you can also beat me and punish me for having genuine feelings. If your music is not a deception, if it really is expressing the truth, then I have every right to expect you to respect the feelings of your child. Otherwise there is something wrong, and the music I have absorbed through every pore is a lie. I want to shout it out to all the world in order to keep others—for example, my little brother and sister—from becoming the victims of your seduction. If your theology, your sermons, your words have been telling the truth, you would have to treat me very differently. You wouldn't be able to watch my suffering uncomprehendingly, for I am 'the neighbor' you're supposed to love. You wouldn't punish me for my tears, wouldn't make me bear my distress all alone without helping me, wouldn't forbid me to speak, if you were an honest and trustworthy man. After all that's been done to me, I think your ideas of goodness, neighborly love, and redemption are empty and false; everything I used to believe is nothing but theatrics; there is nothing real about it. What I experience is real, and what you have said must be able to be measured against my reality. But when the measurement is taken, your words prove to be pure playacting. You enjoy having a child who listens to you and admires you. It satisfies your needs. The others don't notice this and think you really have something to offer them. But *I* noticed. I guessed your state of neediness, but I wasn't allowed to say anything about it."

The boy wasn't allowed to say this to his father. But

as an adult he said it to Richard Wagner. He wrote it in no uncertain terms, and the world took what he wrote seriously. Neither Nietzsche nor "the world," unfortunately, wondered about its source. Thus both missed the important point.

NIETZSCHE THE WOMAN HATER

In contrast to the general validity of Nietzsche's censure of the Wagner phenomenon, of middle-class cultural values and Christian moral values, his ideas about "the nature of woman" often seem grotesquely distorted, but only if we are unaware of the actual women who gave rise to them. As a child, Nietzsche was surrounded by women intent on bringing him up correctly, and he had to use all his energies to endure this situation. He paid them back in later years, but only on a symbolic level, by attacking *all* women—except his mother and sister. The women who actually caused his suffering remained unassailable, at the cost of the loss of objectivity.

Nietzsche's misogyny becomes understandable, of course, if we consider how much distrust must have accumulated in someone who was whipped so frequently as a child. But this doesn't authorize him as an adult to write in his blind and irresponsible rage: "You are going to women? Do not forget the whip!" There is no doubt that Nietzsche was brought up according to the principles of "poisonous pedagogy" described extensively in my previous books. The documents I cite in *For Your Own Good* illustrate how children must be tricked, deceived, and manipulated to make them pious and good.

That is why Nietzsche was rarely able to show his discontent at his sister's manipulative and insincere behavior toward him, why he didn't allow himself to see her as she really was. If he ever did see the truth, he quickly retracted anything he may have said against her. Although he admitted on one occasion that he could not stand her voice, he immediately added that basically he had never really doubted her goodwill, her intentions, her love for him, or her trustworthiness. How could he, since he had only one sister and wanted to believe absolutely that she loved him and that her love was more than exploitation and a need to win recognition at any price. If he had been able to see *the way the women in his childhood really were*, then it would not have been necessary for him to generalize by making *all* women into witches and serpents and to hate them all.

FASCISM (*The Blond Beast*)

It is not my intention here to explain Nietzsche's life in terms of his childhood but rather to understand the function of his philosophy in his struggle against the pain stemming from his childhood. His formative experience consisted in *contempt for the weak and obedience toward those wielding power*. This seemingly innocuous combina-

Friedrich Nietzsche as an Infantryman in Naumburg, 1868
Ullstein Bilderdienst

tion, familiar to so many of us from childhood, is the nucleus of every fascist ideology. As a result of having been treated brutally in childhood, fascists of whatever stamp will blindly accept their leader and treat those weaker than themselves brutally. The fact that this behavior can be accompanied by a longing for the release of creative powers that the methods of "poisonous pedagogy" suppress in every child is to be seen very plainly in Nietzsche and others and also in certain statements by C. G. Jung. The human being's need to live and to be allowed to develop freely is coupled with the former persecutor's introjected voice. Just as the child's cries were once smothered by the principles of "poisonous pedagogy," so too the call to life is smothered by the brutality of fascism. The introjected system allies itself with the child's own wishes and leads to destructive ideologies that can have a fascination for anyone who experienced a cruel upbringing. Thus, it is not Nietzsche's writings that are dangerous but the child-rearing system of which he and his readers were the product. The Nazis were able to transform what seemed to be his *life-affirming philosophy* into a *death-affirming ideology* because it was never in its essence separate from death.

It is not by chance that *Thus Spake Zarathustra* became Nietzsche's most famous work, for his puzzled readers at least found in Zarathustra's way of speaking a frame of reference familiar to them since childhood: the rhetorical style of the preacher. How familiar, too, although clothed in novel words, was the struggle for life in the face of the deadening requirement to be obedient. Again and again Nietzsche circles around this dichotomy.

> I pursued the living; I walked the widest and the narrowest paths that I might know its nature. With a hundredfold mirror I still caught its glance *when its mouth was* closed, so that its eyes might speak to me. And its eyes spoke to me. [Italics mine]
>
> But wherever I *found the living*, there I heard also the *speech on obedience*. Whatever lives, obeys. [Italics mine]
>
> And this is the second point: he who cannot obey himself is commanded. That is the nature of the living.
>
> This, however, is the third point that I heard: that commanding is harder than obeying; and not only because he who commands must carry the burden of all who obey, and because this burden may easily crush him. An experiment and hazard appeared to me to be in all commanding; and whenever the living commands, it hazards itself. Indeed, even when it commands *itself*, it must still pay for its commanding. It must become the judge, the avenger, and the victim of its own law. How does this happen? I asked myself. What persuades the living to obey and command, and to practice obedience even when it commands? . . .
>
> And life itself confided this secret to me: "Behold," it said, "I am *that which must always overcome itself*. Indeed, you call it a will to procreate or a drive to an end, to something higher, farther, more manifold: but all this is one, and one secret.
>
> "Rather would I perish than forswear this; and verily, where there is perishing and a falling of leaves, behold, there life sacrifices itself—for power. That I must be struggle and a becoming and an end and an opposition to ends

—alas, whoever guesses what is my will should also guess on what *crooked* paths it must proceed.

"Whatever I create and however much I love it—soon I must oppose it and my love; thus my will wills it. And you too, lover of knowledge, are only a path and footprint of my will; verily, my will to power walks also on the heels of your will to truth.

"Indeed, the truth was not hit by him who shot at it with the word of the 'will to existence': that will does not exist. For, what does not exist cannot will; but what is in existence, how could that still want existence? Only where there is life is there also will: not will to life but—thus I teach you—will to power.

"There is much that life esteems more highly than life itself; but out of the esteeming itself speaks the will to power."

Thus life once taught me; and with this I shall yet solve the riddle of your heart, you who are wisest.

Verily, I say unto you: good and evil that are not transitory, do not exist. Driven on by themselves, they must overcome themselves again and again. With your values and words of good and evil you do violence when you value; and this is your hidden love and the splendor and trembling and overflowing of your soul. But a more violent force and a new overcoming grow out of your values and break egg and eggshell.

And whoever must be a creator in good and evil, verily, he must first be an annihilator and break values. Thus the highest evil belongs to the highest goodness: but this is creative.

Let us speak of this, you who are wisest, even if it be bad. *Silence is worse; all truths that are kept silent become poisonous.* [Italics mine]

And may everything be broken that cannot brook our truths! There are yet many houses to be built!

Thus spoke Zarathustra.

How wicked and hard a child must feel who remains true to himself and does not betray what he perceives and sees. How difficult and at the same time how essential it is to be able to say no.

> With the storm that is called "spirit" I blew over your wavy sea; I blew all clouds away; I even strangled the strangler that is called "sin."
>
> O my soul, I gave you the right *to say No like the storm, and to say Yes as the clear sky says Yes*: now you are still as light whether you stand or *walk through storms of negation*. [Italics mine]
>
> O my soul, I gave you back the freedom over the created and uncreated; and who knows, as you know, the voluptuous delight of what is yet to come?
>
> O my soul, I taught you the contempt that does not come like the worm's gnawing, the great, *the loving contempt that loves most where it despises most*. [Italics mine]
>
> O my soul, I taught you to persuade so well that you persuade the very ground—like the sun who persuades even the sea to his own height.
>
> O my soul, I took from you all obeying, knee-bending, and "Lord"-saying; I myself gave you the name "cessation of need" and "destiny."

But the life the child seeks is fraught with danger, the loveliest fantasies dimmed by early experiences and threats.

My heels twitched, then my toes hearkened to understand you, and rose: for the dancer has his ear in his toes.

I leaped toward you, but you fled back from my leap, and the tongue of your fleeing, flying hair licked me in its sweep.

Away from you I leaped, and from your serpents' ire; and already you stood there, half turned, your eyes full of desire.

With crooked glances you teach me—crooked ways; on crooked ways my foot learns treachery. [Italics mine]

I fear you near, I love you far; your flight lures me, your seeking cures me: I suffer, but what would I not gladly suffer for you?

You, whose coldness fires, whose hatred seduces, whose flight binds, whose scorn inspires:

Who would not hate you, you great *binder, entwiner, temptress, seeker, and finder?* Who would not love you, you innocent, impatient, wind-swift, *child-eyed* sinner? [Italics mine]

Whereto are you luring me now, you never-tame extreme? And now you are fleeing from me again, you sweet wildcat and ingrate!

I dance after you, I follow wherever your traces linger. Where are you? Give me your hand! Or only one finger!

Here are caves and thickets; we shall get lost. Stop! Stand still! Don't you see owls and bats whirring past?

You owl! You bat! Intent to confound! Where are we? Such howling and yelping you have learned from a hound.

Your lovely little white teeth are gnashing at me; out of a curly little mane your evil eyes are flashing at me.

That is a dance up high and down low: I am the hunter; would you be my dog or my doe?

Alongside me now! And swift, you malicious leaping belle! Now up and over there! Alas, as I leaped I fell.

Oh, see me lying there, you prankster, suing for grace. I should like to walk with you in a lovelier place.

Love's paths through silent bushes, past many-hued plants. Or there along that lake: there goldfish swim and dance.

You are weary now? Over there are sunsets and sheep: when shepherds play on their flutes—is it not lovely to sleep?

You are so terribly weary? I'll carry you there; just let your arms sink. And if you are thirsty—I have got something, but your mouth does not want it to drink.

Oh, this damned nimble, supple snake and slippery witch! Where are you? In my face two red blotches from your hand itch.

I am verily weary of always being your sheepish shepherd. You witch, if *I* have so far sung to you, now you shall cry.

Keeping time with my whip, you shall dance and cry! Or have I forgotten the whip? Not I!

It is permissible to hate and whip the serpent and the witch but not the mother, grandmother, or aunts. In any case, feelings of anger, outrage, and mistrust are unmistakably present here. They may also be directed at "the mob," which has the same symbolic function as the serpent and the witch.

Is this today not the mob's? But the mob does not know what is great, what is small, what is straight and honest: it is innocently crooked, it always lies.

Have a good mistrust today, you higher men, you

stouthearted ones, you openhearted ones! And keep your reasons secret! For this today is the mob's.

What the mob once learned to believe without reasons—who could overthrow that with reasons?

And in the market place one convinces with gestures. But reasons make the mob mistrustful.

And if truth was victorious for once, then ask yourself with good mistrust: "What strong error fought for it?"

Over and over again Nietzsche attempts to find his way out of the mists of confusing moral principles and attain clarity. But his speculating continually obfuscates the truth.

Do not let yourselves be gulled and beguiled! Who, after all, is *your* neighbor? And even if you act "for the neighbor"—you still do not create for him.

Unlearn this "for," you creators! Your very virtue wants that you do nothing "for" and "in order" and "because." You shall plug up your ears against these false little words. "For the neighbor" is only the virtue of the little people: there one says "birds of a feather" and "one hand washes the other." They have neither the right nor the strength for *your* egoism. In your egoism, you creators, is the caution and providence of the pregnant. What no one has yet laid eyes on, the fruit: that your whole love shelters and saves and nourishes. Where your whole love is, with your child, there is also your whole virtue. Your work, your will, that is *your* "neighbor": do not let yourselves be gulled with false values!

The call to war has essentially only one symbolic meaning for Nietzsche: it represents nothing other than declaring battle against the deadly coercion, lies, and cowardice that constricted his life so painfully as a child. But Nietzsche doesn't say it clearly enough, he doesn't reveal the source. That is why he opens the doors to a harmful use of his words.

> A free life is still free for great souls. Verily, *whoever possesses little is possessed that much less*: praised be a little poverty! [Italics mine]
> Only where the state ends, there begins the human being who is not superfluous: there begins the song of necessity, the unique and inimitable tune.
> Where the state *ends*—look there, my brothers! Do you not see it, the rainbow and the bridges of the overman?
> Thus spoke Zarathustra.

And the man who was dependent all his life on his mother and sister writes: "If you would go high, use your own legs. Do not let yourselves be carried up; do not sit on the backs and heads of others." In his own mind, Nietzsche was not sitting on the backs of others, but in his life he allowed the person closest to him to sit on his back to the very end.

On January 14, 1880, he wrote to Malwida von Meysenbug: "For the terrible and almost unceasing martyrdom of my life makes me thirst for the end, and judging by several indications, the stroke that shall deliver me is near enough at hand to allow me to hope." And in 1887 he said these significant words to Paul Deussen: "I don't believe I'm going to last much longer. I'm now near the age when my father died, and I feel I'm going to succumb to the same affliction he had."

The medical diagnosis of the disease that befell Nietzsche at the age of forty-five was "progressive paralysis," and his biographers seem reassured when they "determine" that this later illness "had nothing at all to do" with the illnesses of his school days. And the *118 attacks* in one year (1879) were apparently sheer "coincidence," for in the opinion of many of his biographers, Nietzsche was perfectly healthy until the appearance of his progressive paralysis.

"WHY I AM SO WISE"

Sometimes Nietzsche's words convey something that might be construed as delusions of grandeur and that the reader might easily find offensive. One author has referred to this as Nietzsche's "God complex," and there *are* passages in *Ecce Homo* (1888) and in the letters that actually point to such a complex. How are we to understand this "arrogance" on the part of a thinker as critical and self-critical as Nietzsche? Those who have read the diaries he kept from age twelve to fourteen will scarcely believe that those pages were written by the same person whose later writing they already know—not because the diaries are so childish but because they are so adult. In great part, they could have been written by his aunts, his grandmother, or his father—and in the same style. The writing is colorless and unassuming, as was expected of him. The feelings expressed strike one as inauthentic, weak, sometimes the-atrical, but for the most part false. We sense that what the writer really feels must remain completely beneath the surface without being revealed by a sentence or even a single word.

But this boy, who at twelve wrote like an adult, was also capable of other things. What could he do with his sense of pride, with the certitude that he understood more than those around him? If Nietzsche had expressed his pride at that time, he would have been sinning against an important Christian virtue, humility. He certainly would have met with disapproval and indignation. The boy there-fore was forced to suppress his healthy and understandable feeling of joy at what he knew as well as his grief at being alone with his knowledge; not until much later—in *Ecce Homo*, for instance—was he able to express these feelings. But then he did it in a way that people could not tolerate, putting himself in the position of a "sinner," of someone who violates society's norms—the norm of modesty, for one. He was sure to reap the moral indignation of his contemporaries and of posterity, an outcome he accepted gladly, presumably even enjoyed, because he felt liberated by his daring. A different kind of liberation, such as having insights that could be shared with others, was unknown to him. This man who was condemned to be alone with his insights never learned that someone can speak the truth without punishing himself for it and without giving others grounds for dismissing what he says by applying the label "delusions of grandeur."

But what strikes us as delusions of grandeur in

Nietzsche presumably has other roots than simply an inner compulsion to provoke others. Nietzsche was the firstborn child, and even after the birth of his sister he could not count on anyone sharing his experiences and perceptions with him, especially those connected with the change brought about in his father by illness. He therefore found himself alone with his discoveries and was deprived of the reassurance that it would be safe to share them with those close to him. If he had had older siblings, perhaps his perceptions would not have had such disastrous consequences for him. Perhaps he could at least have counted on an occasional understanding glance from an older brother or sister. As it was, however, he was always *alone* with his awareness, which in his case meant *abandoned* with his awareness, a situation that does not necessarily evoke feelings of pride but can also cause pain.

The many passages in which Nietzsche characterizes Christianity are a key to how he felt about his relatives. We need only substitute "my aunts" or "my family" for the word "Christianity" for his vehement attacks suddenly to make sense.

In Christianity the instincts of the subjugated and oppressed come to the fore: here the lowest classes seek their salvation. The casuistry of sin, self-criticism, the inquisition of the conscience, are pursued as a *pastime*, as a remedy for boredom; the emotional reaction to one who has *power*, called "God," is constantly sustained (by means of prayer); and what is highest is considered unattainable, a gift, "grace." Public acts are precluded; the hiding-place, the darkened room, is Christian. The body is despised, hygiene repudiated as sensuality; the church even opposes cleanliness (the first Christian measure after the expulsion of the Moors was the closing of the public baths, of which there were two hundred and seventy in Cordova alone). Christian too is a certain sense of cruelty against oneself and against others; hatred of all who think differently; the will to persecute. Gloomy and exciting conceptions predominate; the most highly desired states, designated with the highest names, are epileptoid; the diet is so chosen as to favor morbid phenomena and overstimulate the nerves. Christian too is mortal enmity against the lords of the earth, against the "noble"—along with a sly, secret rivalry (one leaves them the "body," one wants *only* the "soul"). Christian, finally, is the hatred of the *spirit*, of pride, courage, freedom, liberty of the spirit; Christian is the hatred of the *senses*, of joy in the senses, of joy itself.

It is not difficult to imagine how much Nietzsche suffered as a child because of his family's beliefs and assertions, because of their rejection of his bodily needs and his physical self, and because of their constant moral dictates, such as repentence, piety, neighborly love, chastity, loyalty, purity, and devotion. He regarded them—and rightly so—as empty concepts conflicting with everything that meant life for him, as for every child, and standing for "*hatred* of the natural (of reality!)." Nietzsche saw the Christian world as a fictitious one, as "the expression of a profound vexation at the sight of reality. *But this explains everything*. Who alone has good reason to lie his way out of reality? He who suffers from it. But to suffer from reality is to be a piece of reality that has come to grief."

Couldn't these words also be the child's speculations about his do-good maiden aunts, whose main concern in raising the boy was to destroy the vitality in him that had also been destroyed in them? If we see the principles of his own upbringing behind his description of Christianity's hypocritical morality, then we can easily recognize in the self-proclaimed representative of the "noble lords of the earth" the child who is still rooted in his feelings and is therefore strong, vital, and sincere but also in danger of having to sacrifice his vitality to pedagogical principles. When we read *The Antichrist* with this key in mind, passages that were previously perplexing now gain a clear meaning.

> If, for example, it makes men happy to believe that they have been redeemed from sin, it is not necessary, as a condition for this, that man is, in fact, sinful, but merely that he feels sinful. And if faith is quite generally needed above all, then reason, knowledge, and inquiry must be discredited: the way to truth becomes the *forbidden* way.
>
> Strong *hope* is a far more powerful stimulant of life than any single realization of happiness could ever be. Those who suffer must be sustained by a hope that can never be contradicted by any reality or be disposed of by any fulfillment—a hope for the beyond.

> So that it could say No to everything on earth that represents the ascending tendency of life, to that which has turned out well, to power, to beauty, to self-affirmation, the instinct of *ressentiment*, which had here become genius, had to invent *another* world from whose point of

view this affirmation of life appeared as evil, as the reprehensible as such.

Psychologically considered, "sins" become indispensable in any society organized by priests: they are the real handles of power. The priest *lives* on sins, it is essential for him that people "sin." Supreme principle: "God forgives those who repent"—in plain language: those who submit to the priest.

The tone becomes different when Nietzsche speaks about the man Jesus.

To repeat, I am against any attempt to introduce the fanatic into the Redeemer type: the word *impérieux*, which Renan uses, is alone enough to annul the type. The "glad tidings" are precisely that there are no longer any opposites; the kingdom of heaven belongs to the *children*; the faith which finds expression here is not a faith attained through struggle—it is there, it has been there from the beginning; it is, as it were, an infantilism that has receded into the spiritual. The case of puberty being retarded and not developing in the organism, as a consequence of degeneration, is well known, at least to physiologists. Such a faith is not angry, does not reproach, does not resist: it does not bring "the sword"—it simply does not foresee how it might one day separate. It does not prove itself either by miracle or by reward and promise, least of all "by scripture": at every moment it is its own miracle, its own reward, its own proof, its own "kingdom of God." Nor does this faith formulate itself: it *lives*, it resists all formulas.

His affirmation of the Redeemer does not, however, prevent him from expressing his disgust for the church and its priests.

> The concepts "beyond," "Last Judgment," "immortality of the soul," and "soul" itself are instruments of torture, systems of cruelties by virtue of which the priest became master, remained master.
> Everybody knows this, *and yet everything continues as before*.

From the beginning, he says, the priests used Jesus to attain power for themselves.

> In Paul the priest wanted power once again—he could use only concepts, doctrines, symbols with which one tyrannizes masses and forms herds. What was the one thing that Mohammed later borrowed from Christianity? Paul's invention, his means to priestly tyranny, to herd formation: the faith in immortality—*that is, the doctrine of the "judgment."*

> The great lie of personal immortality destroys all reason, everything natural in the instincts—whatever in the instincts is beneficent and life-promoting or guarantees a future now arouses mistrust. To live so, that there is not longer any *sense* in living, that now becomes the "sense" of life. . . . that little prigs and three-quarter-madmen may have the conceit that the laws of nature are constantly broken for their sakes—such an intensification of every kind of selfishness into the infinite, into the *impertinent,*

cannot be branded with too much contempt. And yet Christianity owes its triumph to this miserable flattery of personal vanity.

The priest knows only one great danger: that is science, the sound conception of cause and effect. . . . Man *shall not* look outside, he shall look into himself; he *shall not* look into things cleverly and cautiously, like a learner, he shall not look at all—he shall *suffer*. And he shall suffer in such a way that he has need of the priest at all times. . . . A *priestly* attempt! . . .

When the natural consequences of a deed are no longer "natural," but thought of an caused by the conceptual specters of superstition, by "God," by "spirits," by "souls," as if they were merely "moral" consequences, as reward, punishment, hint, means of education, then the presupposition of knowledge has been destroyed—

I have selected these quotations with various perspectives in mind. In addition to expressing clearly the adult Nietzsche's feelings about Christianity, they also convey to alert readers his unconscious feelings, repressed since childhood, toward his first attachment figures. These passages reveal as well the child-raising methods and principles Nietzsche must have been exposed to as a child without being able to call them by name: above all, contempt for everything vital, sensual, and creative; the struggle to replace the child's feeling of well-being with guilt feelings and repentence; the suppression of his ability to think for himself, of his critical capacities, of his need to understand connections (the intellectual disciplines), and of his need for freedom and spontaneity. Not only obedience and submissiveness were preached to him but also the so-called love of truth, which was pure hypocrisy, for the boy who was forbidden to say anything critical was also forced to lie repeatedly. It is this perversion of values that continually aroused Nietzsche's ire and that he tried to make tangible by his paradoxical formulations in the hope that he would no longer have to be alone with his anger.

THE GLORIFICATION OF EVIL
(Vitality Is Evil)

Nietzsche considered himself the advocate of evil in only one specific connection: where evil is seen as the opposite of what people *call* good. He writes:

> When the herd animal is irradiated by the glory of the purest virtue, the exceptional man must have been devaluated into evil. When mendaciousness at any price monopolizes the word "truth" for its perspective, the really truthful man is bound to be branded with the worst names.

And a few lines earlier he quotes Zarathustra:

> "False coasts and assurances the good have taught you; in the lies of the good you were hatched and huddled. Everything has been made fraudulent and has been twisted through and through by the good."
>
> "The good are unable to *create*; they are always the

beginning of the end; they crucify him who writes new values on new tablets; they sacrifice the future to *themselves*—they sacrifice all man's future."

"The good have always been the beginning of the end."

"And whatever harm those do who slander the world, the harm done by the good is the most harmful harm."

That these observations derive from Nietzsche's childhood experiences is corroborated by the following passage:

> The condition of the existence of the good is the *lie*: put differently, not *wanting* to see at any price how reality is constituted fundamentally—namely, not in such a way as to elicit benevolent instincts at all times, and even less in such a way as to tolerate at all times the interference of those who are myopically good-natured.

This awareness leads to boundless loneliness, which was the fate of this man from the beginning. The more he came to understand his environment, the more isolated he felt because he couldn't communicate his insights and experiences to anyone. After he finally attempted to communicate them in *Thus Spake Zarathustra*, only to find that his hopes of being understood and of finding acceptance for his ideas had been in vain, he wrote these words in *Ecce Homo*:

> Except for these ten-day works, the years during and above all *after* my *Zarathustra* were marked by distress with-

out equal. One pays dearly for immortality: one has to die several times while still alive.

There is something I call the *rancune* of what is great: everything great—a work, a deed—is no sooner accomplished than it turns *against* the man who did it. By doing it, he has become *weak*; he no longer endures his deed, he can no longer face it. Something one was never permitted to will lies *behind* one, something in which the knot in the destiny of humanity is tied—and now one labors *under* it!— It almost crushes one.— The *rancune* of what is great.

Then there is the gruesome silence one hears all around one. Solitude has seven skins; nothing penetrates them any more. One comes to men, one greets friends—more desolation, no eye offers a greeting. At best, a kind of revolt. Such revolts I experienced, very different in degree but from almost everybody who was close to me. It seems nothing offends more deeply than suddenly letting others feel a distance; those *nobel* natures who do not know how to live without reverence are rare.

Thirdly, there is the absurd sensitivity of the skin to small stings, a kind of helplessness against everything small. This seems to me to be due to the tremendous squandering of all defensive energies which is a presupposition of every *creative* deed, every deed that issues from one's most authentic, inmost, nethermost regions. Our *small* defensive capacitites are thus, as it were, suspended; no energy is left for them.

I still dare to hint that one digests less well, does not like to move, is all too susceptible to feeling chills as well as mistrust—mistrust that is in many instances merely an etiological blunder. In such a state I once sensed the proximity of a herd of cows even before I saw it, merely because milder and more philanthropic thoughts came back to me: *they* had warmth.

Nietzsche's loneliness was caused by his inner plight, for only the very few were receptive to what he said, and perhaps he wasn't aware of even these few. Thus, he would rather be alone than together with people who did not understand him. In his solitude, he had new ideas and made new discoveries; since they were based on his most personal experiences, but at the same time concealed them, they were difficult to share with others, and they only deepened his loneliness and the gulf between him and those around him. It was a process that had already begun in childhood, a childhood consisting of his continually being the giver. The boy's *raison d'être* was to understand others, to be patient with them, to overlook their failings, and to validate their self-esteem but never to appease his own hunger to be understood. In "Night Song," Nietzsche describes the tragedy of his attempt to find a solution, the tragedy of the person who gives and who thirsts:

> Light am I; ah, that I were night! But this is my loneliness that I am girt with light. Ah, that I were dark and nocturnal! How I could suck at the breasts of light! And even you would I bless, you little sparkling stars and glowworms up there, and be overjoyed with your gifts of light.
>
> But I live in my own light; I drink back into myself the flames that break out of me. I do not know the happiness of those who receive; and I have often dreamed that even

Friedrich Nietzsche

stealing must be more blessed than receiving. This is my poverty, that my hand never rests from giving; this is my envy, that I see waiting eyes and the lit-up nights of longing. Oh, wretchedness of all givers! Oh, darkening of my sun! Oh, craving to crave! Oh, ravenous hunger in satiation!

They receive from me, but do I touch their souls? There is a cleft between giving and receiving; and the narrowest cleft is the last to be bridged. A hunger grows out of my beauty: I should like to hurt those for whom I shine; I should like to rob those to whom I give; thus do I hunger for malice. To withdraw my hand when the other hand already reaches out to it; to linger like the waterfall, which lingers even while it plunges: thus do I hunger for malice. Such revenge my fullness plots: such spite wells up out of my loneliness. My happiness in giving died in giving; my virtue tired of itself in its overflow.

This text speaks of the envy directed at those who are able to take, who received love as a child, who can feel secure in a group, who are not condemned to open up new worlds in their loneliness, bestowing those worlds on others and reaping hostility in return. But fate cannot be changed. Those who do not want to live without the truth must also endure the cold regions of loneliness. Nietzsche writes:

How much truth does a spirit *endure*, how much truth does it *dare*? More and more that became for me the real measure of value. Error (faith in the ideal) is not blindness, error is *cowardice*.

Every attainment, every step forward in knowledge,

follows from courage, from hardness against oneself, from cleanliness in relation to oneself.

I do not refute ideals, I merely put on gloves before them.

Nitimur in vetitum: in this sign my philosophy will triumph one day, for what one has forbidden so far as a matter of principle has always been—truth alone.

"For what one has forbidden so far as a matter of principle has always been—truth alone." These words are valid for the history of humankind as well as for Nietzsche's family. And because he was no longer willing or able to comply with this prohibition, he sought refuge in atheism. He did not want to parrot religious platitudes.

"God," "immortality of the soul," "redemption," "beyond"—without exception, concepts to which I never devoted any attention, or time; not even as a child. Perhaps I have never been child-like enough for them?

I do not by any means know atheism as a result; even less as an event: it is a matter of course with me, from instinct. I am too inquisitive, too *questionable*, too exuberant to stand for any gross answer. God is a gross answer, an indelicacy against us thinkers—at bottom merely a gross prohibition for us: you shall not think!

Every evening after saying his prayers and before going to sleep, the little boy tried to make himself remember not to think. This prohibition was directed against life, for the vitality of thoughts is destroyed if one is constantly checking and sorting them out to see if they are permitted or forbidden for the sake of adapting them to dogma.

This ultimate, most joyous, most wantonly extravagant Yes to life represents not only the highest insight but also the *deepest*, that which is most strictly confirmed and born out by truth and science. Nothing in existence may be subtracted, nothing is dispensable—those aspects of existence which Christians and other nihilists repudiate are actually on an infinitely higher level in the order of rank among values than that which the instinct of decadence could approve and call good. To comprehend this requires courage and, as a condition of that, an excess of strength: for precisely as far as courage may venture forward, precisely according to that measure of strength one approaches the truth. Knowledge, saying Yes to reality, is just as necessary for the strong as cowardice and the flight from reality—as the "ideal" is for the weak, who are inspired by weakness.

They are not free to know: the decadents *need* the lie—it is one of the conditions of their preservation.

Whoever does not merely comprehend the word "Dionysian" but comprehends *himself* in the word "Dionysian" needs no refutation of Plato or Christianity or Schopenhauer—he *smells the decay*.

For a physiologist such a juxtaposition of values simply leaves no doubt. When the least organ in an organism fails, however slightly, to enforce with complete assurance its self-preservation, its "egoism," restitution of its energies—the whole degenerates. The physiologist demands *excision* of the degenerating part; he denies all solidarity with what degenerates; he is worlds removed from pity for it. But the priest desires precisely the degeneration of the whole, of humanity: for that reason, he *conserves* what degenerates—at this price he rules.

When seriousness is deflected from the self-preservation and the enhancement of the strength of the body—*that is, of life*—when anemia is construed as an ideal, and contempt for the body as "salvation of the soul"—what else is this if not a *recipe* for decadence?

The loss of the center of gravity, resistance to the natural instincts—in one word, "selflessness"—that is what was hitherto called *morality*.— With the *Dawn* I first took up the fight against the morality that would unself man.

Nietzsche was of the opinion that the Renaissance was Western civilization's great opportunity to free itself from Christianity's life-denying moral system and that this opportunity was lost because of Luther.

Luther, this calamity of a monk, restored the church and, what is a thousand times worse, Christianity, at the very moment *when it was vanquished.*—Christianity, this denial of the will to life become religion!—Luther, an impossible monk who, on account of his own "impossibility," attacked the church and—consequently—restored it.— The Catholics would have good reason to celebrate Luther festivals, to write Luther plays.— Luther—and the "moral rebirth"!

The morality that would un-self man is the morality of decline *par excellence*—the fact, "I am declining," trans-

posed into the imperative, "all of you *ought* to decline"—
and not only into the imperative.— This only morality that
has been taught so far, that of un-selfing, reveals a will to
the end; fundamentally, it negates life.

This would still leave open the possibility that not
humanity is degenerating but only that parasitical type of
man—that of the *priest*—which has used morality to raise
itself mendaciously to the position of determining human
values—finding in Christian morality the means to come
to *power*.— Indeed, this is *my* insight: the teachers, the
leaders of humanity, theologians all of them, were also, all
of them, decadents: *hence* the revaluation of all values into
hostility to life, *hence* morality—

Definition of morality: Morality—the idiosyncrasy of
decadents, with the ulterior motive of revenging oneself
against life—successfully. I attach value to this definition.

Have I been understood?— I have not said one word
here that I did not say five years ago through the mouth
of Zarathustra.

The uncovering of Christian morality is an event
without parallel, a real catastrophe. He that is enlightened
about that, is a *force majeure*, a destiny—he breaks the
history of mankind in two. One lives before him, or one
lives after him.

The lightning bolt of truth struck precisely what was
highest so far: let whoever comprehends *what* has here been
destroyed see whether anything is left in his hands. Everything that has hitherto been called "truth" has been recognized as the most harmful, insidious, and subterranean
form of lie; the holy pretext of "improving" mankind, as
the ruse for sucking the blood of life itself. Morality as
vampirism.

Whoever uncovers morality also uncovers the disvalue

of all values that are and have been believed; he no longer see anything venerable in the most venerated types of man, even in those pronounced holy; he considers them the most calamitous type of abortion—calamitous because they exerted such fascination.

The concept of "God" invented as a counterconcept of life—everything harmful, poisonous, slanderous, the whole hostility unto death against life synthesized in this concept in a gruesome unity! The concept of the "beyond," the "true world" invented in order to devaluate the only world there is—in order to retain no goal, no reason, no task for our earthly reality! The concept of the "soul," the "spirit," finally even *immortal* soul," invented in order to despise the body, to make it sick, "holy"; to oppose with a ghastly levity everything that deserves to be taken seriously in life, the questions of nourishment, abode, spiritual diet, treatment of the sick, cleanliness, and weather.

In place of health, the "salvation of the soul"—that is, a *folie circulaire* between penitential convulsions and hysteria about redemption. The concept of "sin" invented along with the torture instrument that belongs with it, the concept of "free will," in order to confuse the instincts, to make mistrust of the instincts second nature. In the concept of the "selfless," the "self-denier," the distinctive sign of decadence, feeling attracted by what is harmful, being unable to find any longer what profits one, self-destruction is turned into the sign of value itself, into "duty," into "holiness," into what is "divine" in man. Finally—this is what is most terrible of all—the concept of the *good* man signifies that one sides with all that is weak, sick, failure, suffering of itself—all that ought to perish: the principle of selection is crossed—an ideal is fabricated from the contradiction against the proud and well-turned-out human

being who says Yes, who is sure of the future, who guar-
antees the future—and he is now called *evil*.— And all
this was believed, *as morality!*— *Ecrasez l'infâme!*—

If we didn't already know that Nietzsche's forebears
on both sides were theologians for several generations back,
the following words would at least indicate that Nietzsche's
outburst is not simply a philosopher's mental gymnastics
but the bitter earnest produced by vivid, first-hand experiences.

> It is necessary to say whom we consider our antithesis:
> it is the theologians and whatever has theologians' blood
> in its veins—and that includes our whole philosophy.
> Whoever has seen this catastrophe at close range or,
> better yet, been subjected to it and almost perished of it,
> will no longer consider it a joking matter.

Not until he was an adult did Nietzsche read the
books by the theologians. But his hatred of "the lie" has
deeper roots and is connected with his hatred of the women
who passed his theological heritage on to him as a child.

> May I here venture the surmise that I *know* women?
> That is part of my Dionysian dowry. Who knows? Perhaps
> I am the first psychologist of the eternally feminine. They
> all love me—an old story—not counting *abortive* females,
> the "emancipated" who lack the stuff for children.— For-
> tunately, I am not willing to be torn to pieces: the perfect
> woman tears to pieces when she loves.— I know these
> charming maenads.— Ah, what a dangerous, creeping,

subterranean little beast of prey she is! And yet so agreeable!— A little woman who pursues her revenge would run over fate itself.—Woman is indescribably more evil than man; also cleverer: good nature is in a woman a form of degeneration.— In all so-called "beautiful souls" something is physiologically askew at bottom; I do not say everything, else I should become medi-cynical. The fight for equal rights is actually a symptom of a disease: every physician knows that.—Woman, the more she is a woman, resists rights in general hand and foot: after all, the state of nature, the eternal war between the sexes, gives her by far the first rank.

But the furious child doesn't stop with women; he also attacks their idol. For everything they did to him happened in the name of God.

The Christian conception of God—God as god of the sick, God as a spider, God as spirit—is one of the most corrupt conceptions of the divine ever attained on earth. It may even represent the low-water mark in the descending development of divine types. God degenerated into the *contradiction* of life, instead of being its transfiguration and eternal Yes! God as the declaration of war against life, against nature, against the will to live! God—the formula for every slander against "this world," for every lie about the "beyond"! God—the deification of nothingness, the will to nothingness pronounced holy!

Nietzsche was not permitted to vent his feelings—of rage, indignation, vindictiveness, mockery, and contempt, which were caused by concrete, tragic experiences—on those who made him suffer. In his intellectual prison he could attack only ideas or people in the abstract, such as, for example, "women."

Although it is not difficult for us to recognize which experiences incited his anger, *Nietzsche himself* was not conscious of its source. Thus, he is able to say: "When I wage war against Christianity I am entitled to this because I have never experienced misfortunes and frustrations from that quarter—the most serious Christians have always been well disposed toward me. I myself, an opponent of Christianity *de rigueur*, am far from blaming individuals for the calamity of millennia."

It is tragic that Nietzsche was unable to blame specific individuals for what he observed "in general." For the living roots of his insights, contrary to all appearances, remained concealed from his conscious self. Caught in the labyrinth of his thoughts, he was incapable of locating these roots. The only permissible way out was that he lose his mind.

PHILOSOPHY AS A PROTECTION FROM THE TRUTH

When I hear in Nietzsche's works, especially *The Antichrist*, the cry of the angry child who has never been heard, when I perceive the mute, despairing, but also co-lossal battle that this wounded, highly expressive child waged against the untruthfulness, insensitivity, confusion, stupidity, inconsistency, and weakness of those who raised him, I am by no means relativizing what Nietzsche has to say about Christianity but am simply pointing to its origins. We could ask ourselves the same question that we ask about poets: If Nietzsche had been allowed to experience *consciously* the suffering caused by the way he was brought up, would *The Antichrist* have turned out the way it did? Presumably, he would not have needed to write it in the form he did, as an outpouring of stored-up affect; he surely would have found a different form, appropriate for telling what he had discovered with the aid of his feelings. If it had not been written as an abstract analysis of Christianity but as a document about his own suffering, many readers would have rediscovered themselves in what they read. It would have been an indictment and testimony concerning conditions that people know from experience, but only subliminally. For most people do not have Nietzsche's ability to describe feelings of revulsion, contempt, and disgust with such sensitivity and to justify them so convincingly.

Presumably, the result would then not have been a philosophical work but an autobiographical account that would have opened readers' eyes to reality. Nor would it have been possible to use Nietzsche's writings for a destructive ideology if they had expressed directly all that had befallen him instead of disguising it in symbolic form (as an attack against Christianity in the abstract, for example).

But there was never an opportunity for Nietzsche to

write such a report, since its potential content—which, as it was, he could express only symbolically—was not accessible to his conscious mind, or in any case was not available to him in a direct form. Should our pedagogical system become more relaxed someday, however, should the commandment "Thou shalt not be aware of what was done to you as a child" lose its force, then our heretofore treasured "products of culture" will no doubt decline in number—from unnecessary, useless dissertations all the way to the most famous philosophical treatises. But their place would be taken by many honest reports about what *really* happened to their authors. These documents could give others the courage to see things as they actually are, to call a crime a crime, and to express what they themselves have gone through but have been unable, without any support, to put into words. Reports of this nature would doubtlessly be preferable to complicated speculative writing, for they would serve the crucial purpose of revealing, rather than concealing, the reality of universal human experience.

By establishing the connection between the content, intensity, and power of Nietzsche's thinking and his childhood experiences, I am by no means trying to call his genius into question. Nonetheless, I will probably be accused of this intent, for as a rule the significance of childhood experience is unfortunately minimized and dismissed as of no importance; what *is* seen as important, in this view, is to regard the abstract ideas of "great thinkers," of adults, as pure gold—without any admixture of childhood—and to admire and interpret those ideas at face value. Neither the secondary literature on Nietzsche nor the espousal of his writing by the fascists ever went beyond these limited boundaries.

From my perspective I would say that, on the contrary, most of Nietzsche's writings owe their persuasiveness specifically to his ability to express the experiences he stored up at a very early age. As in the case of Kafka and other great writers, the truth asserts itself so obviously that it is virtually impossible to deny it: the truth of a mistreated child who was not allowed to cry or defend himself. The sudden flashes of insight that can come from reading certain passages in Nietzsche are not the result of the author's power of suggestion but of the strength of experience (although repressed and unconscious) of someone who is telling about what he has suffered and perceived and whose perceptions relate to situations and conditions in which many other people have had to live—or still are living. Nietzsche has this to say about the sources a writer draws from:

> When I seek my ultimate formula for *Shakespeare*, I always find only this: he conceived of the type of Caesar. That sort of thing cannot be guessed: one either is it, or one is not. The great poet dips *only* from his own reality —up to the point where afterward he cannot endure his work any longer.
>
> When I have looked into my *Zarathustra*, I walk up and down in my room for half an hour, unable to master an unbearable fit of sobbing.

If Nietzsche had not been forced to learn as a child that one must master an "unbearable fit of sobbing," if he had simply been *allowed* to sob, then humanity would have been one philosopher poorer, but in return the life of a human being named Nietzsche would have been richer. And who knows what that *vital* Nietzsche would *then* have been able to give humanity?

THREE

The No Longer Avoidable
Confrontation with Facts

1

When Isaac Arises from the Sacrificial Altar

I had been searching for an illustration for the jacket of the British edition of *Thou Shalt Not Be Aware*; I didn't want to leave the selection to chance but thought it important that I myself find an appropriate visual representation of the work's underlying theme. Two Rembrandt depictions of the sacrifice of Isaac—one in Leningrad, the other in Munich—came to mind. In both, the father's hand completely covers the son's face, obstructing his sight, his speech, even his breathing. The main concerns expressed in my book (victimization of the child, the Fourth Commandment admonishing us to honor our parents, and the blindness imposed on children by parents) seemed to find a central focus in Abraham's gesture. Although I was resolved to recommend this detail of Rembrandt's printings to my publisher for the cover, I went to an archive to look at other portrayals of Abraham and Isaac as well. I found thirty in all, done by very dissimilar artists, and with growing astonishment I looked through them one by one.

I had been struck by the fact that in both of the Rembrandt versions I already knew, Abraham is grasping his son's head with his left hand and raising a knife with his right; his eyes, however, are not resting on his son but are turned upward, as though he is asking God if he is carrying out His will correctly. At first I thought that this was Rembrandt's own interpretation and that there must be others, but I was unable to find any. In all the portrayals of this scene that I found, Abraham's face or entire torso is turned away from his son and directed upward. Only his hands are occupied with the sacrifice. As I looked at the pictures, I thought to myself, "The son, an adult at the peak of his manhood, is simply lying there, quietly waiting to be murdered by his father. In some of the versions he is calm and obedient; in only one is he in tears, but not in a single one is he rebellious." In none of the paintings can we detect any questioning in Isaac's eyes, questions such as "Father, why do you want to kill me, why is my life worth nothing to you? Why won't you look at me, why won't you explain what is happening? How can you do this to me? I love you, I trusted in you. Why won't you speak to me? What crime have I committed? What have I done to deserve this?"

Such questions can't even be formulated in Isaac's

mind. They can be asked only by someone who feels himself on equal footing with the person being questioned, only if a dialogue is possible, only if one can look the other in the eye. How can a person lying on a sacrificial altar with hands bound, about to be slaughtered, ask questions when his father's hand keeps him from seeing or speaking and hinders his breathing? Such a person has been turned into an *object*. He has been dehumanized by being made a sacrifice; he no longer has a right to ask questions and will scarcely even be able to articulate them to himself, for there is no room in him for anything besides fear.

As I sat in the archive looking at the pictures, I suddenly saw in them the symbolic representation of our present situation. Inexorably, weapons are being produced for the obvious purpose of destroying the next generation. Yet those who are profiting from the production of these weapons, while enhancing their prestige and power, somehow manage not to think of this ultimate result. Like Abraham, they do not see what their hands are doing, and they devote their entire attention to fulfilling expectations from "above," at the same time ignoring their feelings. They learned to deny their feelings as children; how should they be able to regain the ability to feel now that they are fathers? It's too late for that. Their souls have become rigid, they have learned to adapt. They have also forgotten how to ask questions and how to listen to them. All their efforts are now directed toward creating a situation—war—in which their sons too will be unable to see and hear.

In the face of mobilization for war—even a conventional one, a nonnuclear war—the questions of the younger generation are silenced. To doubt the wisdom of the state is regarded as treason. Any discussion or consideration of alternative possibilities is eliminated at a single stroke. Only practical questions remain: How do we win the war? How do we survive it? Once the point of asking these questions has been reached, the young forget that prosperous and prominent old men have been preparing for war for a long time. The younger generation will march, sing songs, kill and be killed, and they will be under the impression that they are carrying out an extremely important mission. The state will indeed regard highly what they are doing and will reward them with medals of honor, but their souls—the childlike, living, feeling part of their personality—will be condemned to the utmost passivity. They will resemble Isaac as he is always depicted in the sacrificial scene: hands tied, eyes bound, as if it were the most natural thing in the world to wait unquestioningly in this position to be slaughtered by one's father. (In my German translation of the Bible the verb used in this passage is *schlachten*, which refers to the butchering of animals.)

Neither does the father ask any questions. He submits to the divine command as a matter of course, the same way his son submits to him. He must—and wants to—prove that his obedience is stronger than what he calls his love for his child, and as he prepares to carry out the deed his questions vanish. He doesn't ask God for mercy or look for a way out, and if the angel didn't intervene at the last moment, Abraham would become the murderer of his son simply because God's voice demanded it of him. In the pictures I examined, there is no pain to be seen in Abraham's face, no hesitation, no searching, no questioning, no sign that he is conscious of the tragic nature of his situation. All the artists, even Rembrandt, portray him as God's obedient instrument, whose sole concern is to function properly.

It is astonishing at first glance that not one of the artists, each with his own distinct and independent personality, was tempted to give this dramatic scene an individual, personal stamp. Of course the dress, the colors, the surroundings, and the positions of the bodies vary, but the numerous depictions of the scene reveal a remarkably uniform psychological content. An obvious explanation is that all the artists were following the Old Testament text, but we are still justified in asking why. Why wasn't there room in the psyche of these artists for doubt? Why did they all take it for granted that the Bible passage could not be questioned? Why did all of these artists accept the story as valid? The only answer I can think of is that the situation involves a fundamental fact of our existence, with which many of us become familiar during the first years of life and which is so painful that knowledge of it can survive only in the depths of the unconscious. Our awareness of the child's victimization is so deeply rooted in us that we scarcely seem to have reacted at all to the monstrousness of the story of Abraham and Isaac. The moral expressed in the story has almost been accorded the legitimacy of natural law, yet if the result of this legitimacy is something as horrifying as the outbreak of nuclear war, then the moral

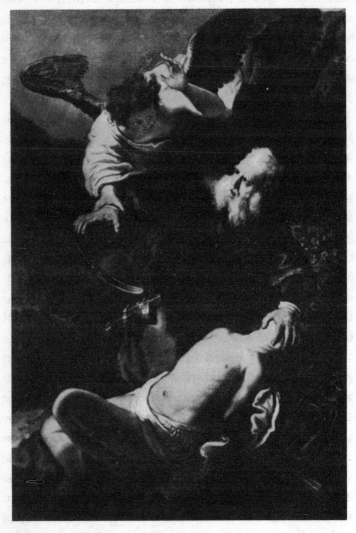

Rembrandt van Rijn, The Sacrifice of Isaac
Archiv für Kunst und Geschichte, Berlin

should not be passively accepted like a natural law but must be questioned. If we love life more than obedience and are not prepared to die in the name of obedience and our fathers' lack of critical judgment, then we can no longer wait like Isaac, with our eyes bound and our hands tied, for our fathers to carry out the will of their fathers.

How, then, can a condition that has endured for millennia be changed? Would it change if the young were to kill off the old so as not to have to go to war? Wouldn't that simply be a forerunner to the horrible war we are trying to prevent, and wouldn't the old situation then be reinforced, the difference being that Abraham's knife would now be in Isaac's hands and the old man would become the victim of the young man? Wouldn't the same cruelty be perpetuated?

But what would happen if Isaac, instead of reaching for the knife, were to use every ounce of his strength to free his hands so that he could remove Abraham's hand from his face? That would change his situation altogether. He would no longer lie there like a sacrificial lamb but would stand up; he would dare to use his eyes and see his father as he really is: uncertain and hesitant yet intent on carrying out a command he does not comprehend. Now Isaac's nose and mouth would be free too, and he could finally draw a deep breath and make use of his voice. He would be able to speak and ask questions, and Abraham, whose left hand could no longer keep his son from seeing and speaking, would have to enter into a dialogue with his son, at the end of which he might possibly encounter the

young man he had once been himself, who was never allowed to ask questions.

And now that the scenario has changed and Isaac can
no longer be counted on to be a victim, there will have to
be a confrontation between the two, a confrontation that
has no conventional precedent but that nevertheless, or
perhaps for this very reason, offers a golden opportunity.
Isaac will ask, "Father, why do you want to kill me?" and
will be given the answer "It is God's will." "Who is God?"
the son will ask. "The great and benevolent Father of us
all, Whom we must obey," Abraham will answer. "Doesn't
it grieve you," the son will want to know, "to have to carry
out this command?" "It is not for me to take my feelings
into account when God orders me to do something." "Then
who are you," Isaac will ask, "if you carry out His orders
without any feeling, and Who is this God, Who can de-
mand such a thing of you?"

It may be that Abraham is too old, that it is too late
for him to perceive the message of life his son is bringing
him, that he will say, "Keep quiet! You understand nothing
of all this." But it may be that he is open to Isaac's questions
because they are his own questions as well, which he has
had to suppress for decades. Even in the former case,
however, the encounter is not doomed to failure as long
as Isaac is unwilling to shut his eyes again but is determined to endure the sight of his father as he really is. If
Isaac refuses to allow himself to be bound and blinded
again for the sake of preserving the illusion of a strong and
wise and benevolent father but instead finds the courage

to look his fallible father in the eye and hear his "Keep quiet" without letting himself be silenced, the confrontation will continue. Then young people will not have to die in wars to preserve the image of their wise fathers. Once young men see what is actually happening, once they become aware that their fathers are steadfastly, unwaveringly, and unthinkingly developing a gigantic weapons system that they hope will not destroy them, although it may their children, then the children will refuse to lie down voluntarily like lambs on the sacrificial altar. But for this to be possible, the children first must be willing to stop obeying the commandment "Thou shalt not be aware."

The commandment itself provides the explanation of why it is so difficult to take that step to awareness. Yet the decision to take it is the first requirement for change. We can still avert our probable fate, provided we do not wait to be rescued by the angel who rewarded Abraham for his obedience. More and more people are refusing to go on playing Isaac's sacrificial role with all its consequences for the future. And perhaps there are also people who reject Abraham's role, who refuse to obey orders that strike them as absurd because they are directed against life. Their ability to ask questions and their refusal to accept senseless answers may signal the beginning of a long overdue reorientation that will help reinforce our Yes to life and No to death. The new Isaac—with his questions, with his awareness, with his refusal to let himself be killed—not only saves his own life but also saves his father from the fate of becoming the unthinking murderer of his child.

Monika Laimgruber, Drawing for Hans Christian Andersen's
The Emperor's New Clothes, *Artemis-Verlag © Monika*
Laimgruber

2

The Emperor's New Clothes

*I*n the preceding chapter, I chose the depictions in art of the sacrifice of Isaac to suggest that it is possible for grown children to have a creative confrontation with their parents. But I do not see the symbolic content of that scene as being limited to the relationship between father and son. Everything I said about Abraham's attitude is equally valid for mothers, and of course Isaac also symbolizes the daughter who can be hindered by both father and mother not only in her movements but also in her ability to see, speak, and breathe.

The assertion that men are solely responsible for conditions in today's world does just as little to expose and combat the presence of evil, destructive rage, violence, and perversion as does the demonization of women. Both sexes have always contributed to the genesis of the forces of evil. Mothers as well as fathers have considered it their duty to punish their children and have used their children to satisfy their own ambitions and other needs. Every aggressive reaction on the child's part to this abuse was suppressed, and this suppression laid the foundation for destructive behavior in adulthood. And yet there must always have been individual parents who were capable of giving love and who provided their children with a counterbalance for the cruelty they suffered. Above all, however, there must have been helping witnesses present—in the person of nannies, household staff, aunts, uncles, siblings, or grandparents—who did not feel responsible for raising the child and who were not camouflaging cruelty as love because they *had* experienced love in their own childhoods. If this were not the case, the human race would have died out long ago. On the other hand, if there had been more mothers and fathers capable of love, our world would be different today; it would be more humane. People would also have a clear understanding of what love is because they would have experienced it in childhood, and it would be inconceivable for biographers to call something an expression of maternal love that in its essence was a prison, concentration camp, refrigerator, or brainwashing institute. Yet according to most of today's biographers, Stalin and Hitler had "loving mothers."

When punishment is held up as proof of love, children

are filled with confusion, which bears bitter fruit later in life. If these children become involved in politics, they continue the work of destruction initiated with them in childhood, and they camouflage it by taking on the role of savior just as their parents did before them. Both Stalin and Hitler claimed that they wanted only to do good. Murder was simply the necessary means to good. This ideology was passed on to them by *both* parents. If this had not been so, if one parent had served as a helping witness and shielded the child from the other parent's brutality and coldness, the children would not have become criminals in later life.

Although it is men who make preparations for war, the confusion in their heads is the end product of child-rearing practices and ways of treating children that are attributable to men *and* women of past generations. The absolute power a mother has over her little child knows no limits, and yet no qualifications are required of her. It is therefore of the utmost urgency to examine more closely the effects of such unchecked power, to recognize parental power for what it is, and, through this awareness, to reduce its danger for the future.

While reflecting on these ideas, I was reminded of the fairy tale "The Emperor's New Clothes." Here a man, the emperor, symbolizes the seemingly mighty but actually helpless parents who are at the same time dangerous because of their total blindness and their great power over their children.

The Emperor's New Clothes

Many, many years ago there was an emperor who was so terribly fond of beautiful new clothes that he spent all his money on his attire. He did not care about his soldiers, or attending the theatre, or even going for a drive in the park, unless it was to show off his new clothes. He had an outfit for every hour of the day. And just as we say, "The king is in his council chamber," his subjects used to say, "The emperor is in his clothes closet."

In the large town where the emperor's palace was, life was gay and happy; and every day new visitors arrived. One day two swindlers came. They told everybody that they were weavers and that they could weave the most marvellous cloth. Not only were the colours and the patterns of their material extraordinarily beautiful, but the cloth had the strange quality of being invisible to anyone who was unfit for his office or unforgivably stupid.

"This is truly marvellous," thought the emperor. "Now if I had robes cut from that material, I should know which of my councillors was unfit for his office, and I would be able to pick out my clever subjects myself. They must weave some material for me!" And he gave the swindlers a lot of money so they could start working at once.

They set up a loom and acted as if they were weaving, but the loom was empty. The fine silk and gold threads they demanded from the emperor they never used, but hid them in their own knapsacks. Late into the night they would sit before their empty loom, pretending to weave.

"I would like to know how far they've come," thought the emperor; but his heart beat strangely when he remembered that those who were stupid or unfit for their office would not be able to see the material. Not that he was

really worried that this would happen to him. Still, it might
be better to send someone else the first time and see how
he fared. Everybody in town had heard about the cloth's
magic quality and most of them could hardly wait to find
out how stupid or unworthy their neighbours were.

"I shall send my faithful prime minister to see the
weavers," thought the emperor. "He will know how to
judge the material, for he is both clever and fit for his
office, if any man is."

The good-natured old man stepped into the room
where the weavers were working and saw the empty loom.
He closed his eyes, and opened them again. "God preserve
me!" he thought. "I cannot see a thing!" But he didn't say
it out loud.

The swindlers asked him to step a little closer so that
he could admire the intricate patterns and marvellous colours of the material they were weaving. They both pointed
to the empty loom, and the poor old prime minister opened
his eyes as wide as he could; but it didn't help, he still
couldn't see anything.

"Am I stupid?" he thought. "I can't believe it, but if
it is so, it is best no one finds out about it. But maybe I
am not fit for my office. No, that is worse, I'd better not
admit that I can't see what they are weaving."

"Tell us what you think of it," demanded one of the
swindlers.

"It is beautiful. It is very lovely," mumbled the old
prime minister, adjusting his glasses. "What patterns!
What colours! I shall tell the emperor that I am greatly
pleased."

"And that pleases us," the weavers said; and now
they described the patterns and told which shades of colour
they had used. The prime minister listened attentively, so

that he could repeat their words to the emperor; and that is exactly what he did.

The two swindlers demanded more money, and more silk and gold thread. They said they had to use it for their weaving, but their loom remained as empty as ever.

Soon the emperor sent another of his trusted councillors to see how the work was progressing. He looked and looked just as the prime minister had, but since there was nothing to be seen, he didn't see anything.

"Isn't it a marvellous piece of material?" asked one of the swindlers; and they both began to describe the beauty of their cloth again.

"I am not stupid," thought the emperor's councillor. "I must be unfit for my office. That is strange; but I'd better not admit it to anyone." And he started to praise the material, which he could not see, for the loveliness of its patterns and colours.

"I think it is the most charming piece of material I have ever seen," declared the councillor to the emperor.

Everyone in town was talking about the marvellous cloth that the swindlers were weaving.

At last the emperor himself decided to see it before it was removed from the loom. Attended by the most important people in the empire, among them the prime minister and the councillor who had been there before, the emperor entered the room where the weavers were weaving furiously on their empty loom.

"Isn't it *magnifique*?" asked the prime minister.

"Your Majesty, look at the colours and the patterns," said the councillor.

And the two old gentlemen pointed to the empty loom, believing that all the rest of the company could see the cloth.

"What!" thought the emperor. "I can't see a thing! Why, this is a disaster! Am I stupid? Am I unfit to be emperor? Oh, it is too horrible!" Aloud he said, "It is very lovely. It has my approval," while he nodded his head and looked at the empty loom.

All the councillors, ministers, and men of great importance who had come with him stared and stared; but they saw no more than the emperor had seen, and they said the same thing that he had said, "It is lovely." And they advised him to have clothes cut and sewn, so that he could wear them in the procession at the next great celebration.

"It is magnificent! Beautiful! Excellent!" All of their mouths agreed, though none of their eyes had seen anything. The two swindlers were decorated and given the title "Royal Knight of the Loom."

The night before the procession, the two swindlers didn't sleep at all. They had sixteen candles lighting up the room where they worked. Everyone could see how busy they were, getting the emperor's new clothes finished. They pretended to take the cloth from the loom; they cut the air with their big scissors, and sewed with needles without thread. At last they announced: "The emperor's clothes are ready!"

Together with his courtiers, the emperor came. The swindlers lifted their arms as if they were holding something in their hands, and said, "These are the trousers. This is the robe, and here is the train. They are all as light as if they were made of spider webs! It will be as if Your Majesty had almost nothing on, but that is their special virtue."

"Oh yes," breathed all the courtiers; but they saw nothing, for there was nothing to be seen.

"Will Your Imperial Majesty be so gracious as to take off your clothes?" asked the swindlers. "Over there by the big mirror, we shall help you put your new ones on."

The emperor did as he was told; and the swindlers acted as if they were dressing him in the clothes they should have made. Finally they tied around his waist the long train which two of his most noble courtiers were to carry.

The emperor stood in front of the mirror admiring the clothes he couldn't see.

"Oh, how they suit you! A perfect fit!" everyone exclaimed. "What colours! What patterns! The new clothes are magnificent!"

"The crimson canopy, under which Your Imperial Majesty is to walk, is waiting outside," said the imperial master of court ceremony.

"Well, I am dressed. Aren't my clothes becoming?" The emperor turned around once more in front of the mirror, pretending to study his finery.

The two gentlemen of the imperial bedchamber fumbled on the floor, trying to find the train which they were supposed to carry. They didn't dare admit that they didn't see anything, so they pretended to pick up the train and held their hands as if they were carrying it.

The emperor walked in the procession under his crimson canopy. And all the people of the town, who had lined the streets or were looking down from the windows, said that the emperor's new clothes were beautiful. "What a magnificent robe! And the train! How well the emperor's clothes suit him!"

None of them were willing to admit that they hadn't seen a thing; for if anyone did, then he was either stupid or unfit for the job he held. Never before had the emperor's clothes been such a success.

"But he doesn't have anything on!" cried a little child.

"Listen to the innocent one," said the proud father. And the people whispered among each other and repeated what the child had said.

"He doesn't have anything on. There's a little child who says that he has nothing on."

"He has nothing on!" shouted all the people at last.

The emperor shivered, for he was certain that they were right; but he thought, "I must bear it until the procession is over." And he walked even more proudly, and the two gentlemen of the imperial bedchamber went on carrying the train that wasn't there.

The belief that older people understand more about life because they supposedly have had more experience was instilled in us at such an early age that we continue to adhere to it even though we know better. Naturally, older craftsmen have more experience in their trades, and older scientists have more facts in their heads, but in both cases their knowledge has precious little to do with wisdom. Nevertheless, most people never give up hoping that they can learn something about life from their elders, whose advanced years must imply richer experience. Even people whose parents have long been dead will seek out parental substitutes such as priests, psychotherapists, gurus, philosophers, or writers, convinced that those who are older must know better, especially if they are famous. They wouldn't have gained recognition, the thinking goes, without some inherent justification for their fame—if the doctrines they proclaim, the values they represent, and the morality they preach didn't have significance for many others too.

And they actually do have significance. Even if the gurus and their disciples are not from the same culture, the repression of childhood experiences is common to all of them, for full awareness of early experiences is taboo in every culture, religion, and system of child-rearing. This situation was not noticed until after World War II, when the first scientifically substantiated reports about childhood appeared, calling into question many of the ideas that had been accepted as right and good for thousands of years. I am thinking here of René Spitz's discovery of hospitalism, John Bowlby's writings about infant abandonment and its consequences, Lloyd De Mause's new look at the history of childhood, Frederick Leboyer's revolutionary discovery that infants already have feelings at birth, and the corroboration provided by primal therapists that feelings repressed in childhood retain their potency and influence our body and mind, often for the rest of our life.

The fact that so many obstetricians still warn today against the dangers of gentle homebirth is attributable not only to their outdated training and the requirements of the hospital system but also to the stunting of their perceptive faculties. They lack the capacity to recognize that a newborn has feelings because such recognition has been blocked for them, possibly as early as the moment of their own birth or perhaps later when their own traumatic experiences are repressed. They examine the newborn infant, and even though they hear its heart-rending cries, they smile at the new mother and tell her that everything is just fine because now the baby's lungs have started to work. These physicians seem to be unaffected by the existing body of knowledge about the role of feelings in the human organism.

The above example of ignorant obstetricians attending childbirth makes clear why advanced age has nothing to do with the value of a person's experiences. Millions of women have given birth in hospitals in recent years under cruel and inhumane conditions, and no one seemed to notice that here a human creature of the tenderest age is being subjected to torture. All that was needed to change this pattern was for one obstetrician, Frederick Leboyer, to take the difficult path of discovering, with the aid of feelings, the memory of his own birth concealed in his psyche and his body. All that was needed was for him to relive his own repressed pain, and suddenly he was able to perceive for the first time what was self-evident: the cries of an infant in the delivery room are expressing pain that is altogether avoidable. To make this simple observation, he first had to overcome the resistance that each of us builds up as a child. We are entitled to this resistance, for we must protect ourselves as best we can from what is unbearable; but what happens when it makes us blind to the most obvious phenomena in our life?

Now computers are being used to help in the care of the newborn, and it has been determined that the child already begins to learn in the first hours of life. Scientists seem to be fascinated by this idea and are busily investigating various achievements of the newborn. But infants also experience feelings and hurt, even prenatally, that set the course for later life, yet these facts haven't attracted the attention of many scientists. It is true that the different functions of the newborn's body can be measured, its behavior observed, the correlates evaluated by the computer. However, as long as the adults involved have not gained access to their own childhood feelings, the infant's feelings, the cause of so many troubles in later life, go totally unnoticed.

What are we to think, then, of the wisdom of older people who had to learn as children that good behavior could be acquired only at the expense of genuine feelings and who were proud of having managed to accomplish this? Since they were not allowed to feel, they became incapable of perceiving vital facts and learning from them. What can these people have to tell us today? They attempt to pass on to the younger generation the same principles their parents once transmitted to them, firmly convinced that they are doing something useful and good. But these are the very principles that destroyed their ability to feel and perceive. Of what use are instructions and moral sermons if one's capacity for feeling and compassion has been lost? The most that will be achieved is to inculcate the absurdest of attitudes, which won't be perceived as such because they are shared by so many.

Thus, politicians can profess to be peace-loving Christians and at the same time advocate the production of weapons *five million times more powerful* than the Hiroshima bomb. These politicians can defend without a qualm the necessity for an absurd arms race because they learned long ago not to feel. It is therefore possible for those caught in this kind of mental system to plan multiple Hiroshima catastrophes and still to pray in church every Sunday for peace; what is more, they consider themselves entitled to bear the responsibility for the fate of the whole world because they are advanced in years, because they have experience with wars, because the last time, forty-five years ago, they took part in one. Yet what now awaits us hasn't the slightest to do with the way the world was forty-five years ago. The wisdom of our fathers, their experience with war and with the destruction of feelings since childhood, can be of little help to us today.

If anything can save us from catastrophe, it is not Abraham, the old man who raises his eyes to heaven and does not see what he is doing. It is his son, who we can only hope has *perhaps* not completely lost his ability to feel and who, owing to this ability, can also imagine the implications of preparing for nuclear war. If Isaac is capable of being horrified at his father's monstrous intent and of *feeling* outraged without repressing this feeling or acting it out, then he will be in a position to understand things that were kept from his father all his life. It is the ability to feel that enables us to establish the right connections, to notice what is going on around us, and to relinquish the illusion that age brings wisdom. Only this painful experience will open Isaac's eyes and make him a man of action instead of a victim. Someone who is not allowed to feel can't learn from experience. Again and again he will accept the so-called wisdom of his elders, which has proven to be unmistakably wrong in our generation—as, for example, "Spare the rod and spoil the child." All his life he will avoid crucial experiences because he must protect himself from pain, and this means ultimately from the truth. He must never doubt his father, must not confront him. Even when his hair has turned white, he will still be his father's obedient child.

Where does such obedience lead? It leads Abraham to the point of murdering his son for the sake of proving his devotion to God the Father, Who requires this act of him. And in our day it leads many old men to prepare for nuclear war with a clear conscience. They destroyed the feeling child in themselves long ago and in doing so learned to kill for the principles of their parents, in good conscience, without remorse and without being able to imagine the suffering of their victims. For a long time we were able to overlook their lack of imagination and their unawareness, thinking "for they know not what they do." But can we still afford to do this when we ourselves, like Isaac, are lying on the sacrificial altar and have not yet completely lost the capacity to imagine what nuclear war would mean? The Isaacs of today, the feeling young sons and daughters, have no alternative but to arise from the altar and confront the psychic reality of fathers preparing for war.

Isaac's actual superiority, if he were to refuse to be made the sacrificial lamb, would be based on his *awareness*, on the fact that *he finds out what his situation is* and clearly recognizes his own need: "I don't want to die for being obedient, and I don't want to kill others. I don't want to let myself be forced to kill by following absurd orders, no matter how cleverly they are packaged or accompanied by threats. I am ready *to look carefully*, to refuse to have my eyes bound any longer, and to find out who really has an interest in my being docile. There must be a way to prevent ourselves from repeating the war games of our fathers, and we now must search for it—without having any models because no models exist for this situation in which we are threatened with nuclear annihilation. We can and we must rely on our own experience and on our desire to create a world in which we can live without having to kill others. Since we want to be true to this desire and not to incomprehensible orders, we are willing to take a careful look around us. We are willing to look closely at the psychic landscape of those who label us naive pacifists. We are willing to examine the sources of their reasoning and to consider whether or not it can be valid for us today."

The cry of the child in Andersen's fairy tale—"But [the emperor] doesn't have anything on!"—awakens people from a mass hypnosis, restores their powers of perception, frees them from the confusion caused by the authorities, and mercilessly exposes the emptiness to which rulers as well as masses have fallen victim. All of this happens suddenly, sparked by the single exclamation of a child. Although these words are enormously liberating, we don't know what to do with our freedom. It is a great relief, to be sure, not to pretend to see the emperor's golden train when, despite our best efforts, we really don't see it—a relief not to have to think we're stupid for not seeing one. But since our fate lies in the emperor's hands, since we have to rely on his wisdom, perceptiveness, and sense of responsibility, our discovery at first fills us with fear. Who will protect us in times of danger? It is now obvious that this emperor can't do it. He appears to be so taken with self-admiration that it would be easy to talk him into doing something foolish. That much seems clear, but only to someone who is not dependent on this emperor. If our future does depend on him, however, *because he is the only one we have*, we would prefer *not* to know what he is really like but would rather believe he will protect us when we are in trouble. For this belief we are ready to sacrifice ourselves, to doubt our own perceptions.

Like children who endure psychic death to preserve the illusion of having an intelligent, foresighted father, soldiers go to war to die for the leader who misuses them. That has been the way of the world, until recently. Many can still remember it, and those who can't are still able to see in films the pageantry surrounding Hitler and the jubilant masses. But it needn't be this way. Indeed, it must not, for the methods of misleading people and destroying them have now taken on gigantic proportions. Therefore, we can no longer afford to deny our perceptions and evade the truth, even if it is painful, for only the truth can save us. It is frightening and painful not to have a strong father when we need his strength. Yet if holding fast to illusion should mean Isaac's death and our destruction today, then the first, imperative step toward turning things around is to relinquish the illusion. Even if this step is fraught with fear, is not even conceivable without fear.

For only a little child can uninhibitedly cry out, "But he doesn't have anything on!" and then only if that child cannot yet assess the consequences of these words. Moreover, the child in Andersen's fairy tale is taken seriously by the father and therefore feels secure. But for adults who never had such a father, the liberation of their senses also endangers or even destroys a vital hope: the hope of being protected. We are horrified at the sight of the deceived emperor without his clothes when we consider that he has the power to issue orders that determine our fate. Of course it would be more conducive to our momentary well-being to deny what we see and to go on believing that the affairs of state are in good hands. But this would be no solution for our future or the future of our children. The Isaac of today can't afford to close his eyes again once he has opened them. Now he knows that his father is not protecting him, and he is determined to protect himself. He is determined not to look away but to examine his situation.

Abraham's upward gaze and his childlike submissiveness are a symbol for numerous experiences Isaac had had earlier without being able to understand them. Likewise, the naive and vain emperor is transformed into a little child who wants to show his father his wonderful new clothes so that the father will finally notice the son. This child, this emperor, could have said, "Father, now that I appear in all my imperial splendor, surrounded by these throngs, you can't overlook me. Now at last you will admire and love me." And the politician who tries to make us believe he has our freedom at heart (even if we should be incinerated by a nuclear bomb), raises his eyes—like Abraham—to his father, who died long ago, and asks like a child: "Haven't I done splendidly? See how well I am representing your values? See how hard I am trying to keep the world the way you described it to me sixty years ago and to keep sacred the values you held dear? See how careful I am not to let anything change, just the way you always wanted? Now are you pleased with me? Now can you love me?" There are many varieties of politicians like this. Perhaps one had a father who always felt he was being persecuted. His son will say to him: "I won't rest until I have destroyed all your enemies. Now are you pleased with me?"

"But what does all that have to do with my fate?" Isaac asks himself. "I can well understand the dealings old men have with their fathers, but I don't want my life to be determined by my forefathers. For what I now have to lose is not real protection but only the illusion of it."

A great many politicians claim they are doing something for us, and we want to believe what they say because we are dependent on them and because the world has become so complicated that we need experts for everything: technical experts, computer experts, and above all safeguards, more and more safeguards so that the world won't fall victim to the bomb. But what is to be done if our fear of the danger that makes such vigilance necessary unceasingly produces new dangers for the simple reason that people who are blocked by their repressed past do not want to look to the future? "What I can try to do now," thinks Isaac, "is direct my father's eyes to me, away from his forebears and to me lying here on the sacrificial altar he has prepared for me. Perhaps that will bring him to his senses, perhaps it won't. But turning my eyes to that altar and to my father has brought *me* to my senses. I am not willing to die, not willing to march and sing war songs. I am not willing to forget that all this has always preceded a war. I have awakened from my millennia-long sleep."

APPENDIX

The Newly Recognized, Shattering Effects of Child Abuse

*F*or some years now there has been proof that the devastating effects of the traumatization of children take their inevitable toll on society. This knowledge concerns every single one of us, and—if disseminated widely enough—should lead to fundamental changes in society, above all to a halt in the blind escalation of violence. The following points are intended to amplify my meaning:

1. All children are born to grow, to develop, to live, to love, and to articulate their needs and feelings for their self-protection.

2. For their development children need the respect and protection of adults who take them seriously, love them, and honestly help them to become oriented in the world.

3. When these vital needs are frustrated and children are instead abused for the sake of adults' needs by being exploited, beaten, punished, taken advantage of, manipulated, neglected, or deceived without the intervention of any witness, then their integrity will be lastingly impaired.

4. The normal reactions to such injury should be anger and pain; since children in this hurtful kind of environment, however, are forbidden to express their anger and since it would be unbearable to experience their pain all alone, they are compelled to suppress their feelings, repress all memory of the trauma, and idealize those guilty of the abuse. Later they will have *no memory of what was done to them*.

5. Disassociated from the original cause, their feelings of anger, helplessness, despair, longing, anxiety, and pain will find expression in destructive acts against others (criminal behavior, mass murder) or against themselves (drug addiction, alcoholism, prostitution, psychic disorders, suicide).

6. If these people become parents, they will then often direct acts of revenge for their mistreatment in childhood against their own children, whom they use as scapegoats. Child abuse is still sanctioned—indeed, held in high regard—in our society as long as it is defined as child-rearing. It is a tragic fact that parents beat their children in order to escape the emotions stemming from how they were treated by their own parents.

7. If mistreated children are not to become criminals or mentally ill, it is essential that *at least once in their life*

they come in contact with a person who knows without any doubt that the environment, not the helpless, battered child, is at fault. In this regard, knowledge or ignorance on the part of society can be instrumental in either saving or destroying a life. Here lies the great opportunity for relatives, social workers, therapists, teachers, doctors, psychiatrists, officials, and nurses *to support the child and to believe her or him*.

8. Till now, society has protected the adult and blamed the victim. It has been abetted in its blindness by theories, still in keeping with the pedagogical principles of our great-grandparents, according to which children are viewed as crafty creatures, dominated by wicked drives, who invent stories and attack their innocent parents or desire them sexually. In reality, children tend to blame themselves for their parents' cruelty and to absolve the parents, whom they invariably love, of all responsibility.

9. For some years now, it has been possible to prove, thanks to the use of new therapeutic methods, that repressed traumatic experiences in childhood are stored up in the body and, although remaining unconscious, exert their influence even in adulthood. In addition, electronic testing of the fetus has revealed a fact previously unknown to most adults: *a child responds to and learns both tenderness and cruelty from the very beginning*.

10. In the light of this new knowledge, even the most absurd behavior reveals its formerly hidden logic once the traumatic experiences of childhood no longer must remain shrouded in darkness.

11. Our sensitization to the cruelty with which children are treated, until now commonly denied, and to the consequences of such treatment will as a matter of course bring to an end the perpetuation of violence from generation to generation.

12. People whose integrity has not been damaged in childhood, who were protected, respected, and treated with honesty by their parents, will be—both in their youth and adulthood—intelligent, responsive, empathic, and highly sensitive. They will take pleasure in life and will not feel any need to kill or even hurt others or themselves. They will use their power to defend themselves but not to attack others. They will not be able to do otherwise than to respect and protect those weaker than themselves, including their children, because this is what they have learned from their own experience and because it is *this* knowledge (and not the experience of cruelty) that has been stored up inside them from the beginning. Such people will be incapable of understanding why earlier generations had to build up a gigantic war industry in order to feel at ease and safe in this world. Since it will not have to be their unconscious life-task to ward off intimidation experienced at a very early age, they will be able to deal with attempts at intimidation in their adult life more rationally and more creatively.

Notes

Notes

PART ONE
Chapter 1

7 "It appears that Picasso's reluctance": Palau i Fabre, *Picasso: The Early Years*, p. 32.

8 "One evening in mid-December 1884": Ibid., p. 29.

9 " 'My father thought it safer' ": Sabartés, *Picasso: An Intimate Portrait*, p. 6.

10 "not to say anything": Ibid., p. 11.

11 "Children's screams screams of women": Wiegand, *Pablo Picasso*, p. 105.

16 "Apparently, Picasso had such a difficult birth": Palau i Fabre, *Picasso: The Early Years*, p. 27.

17 "when taken to school Pablo always": Ibid., p. 31.

Chapter 2

23 "I do not remember much": H. Kollwitz, *The Diary and Letters of Kaethe Kollwitz*, p. 17.

25 "[My] stomach aches were a surrogate": Ibid., p. 17.

25 "On the whole I was quiet": Ibid., pp. 17–18.

25 "I needed to confide": Ibid., p. 23.

25 "There is a picture": Ibid., pp. 18–19.

26 "so that it would all lie behind me": Ibid., p. 20.

26 "I don't know just when I began": Ibid., p. 21.

27 This information held great significance: Miller, *For Your Own Good*, pp. 183–84.

29 Even if there are no dead siblings: Miller, *Prisoners of Childhood*, pp. 3–29.

34 "She often speaks": K. Kollwitz, *Ich sah die Welt mit liebevollen Blicken*, p. 34.

34 "Her awareness that her own child": Ibid., p. 36.

Chapter 3

38 "*My parents were*": Keaton, *My Wonderful World of Slapstick*, p. 14.

38 "A child born backstage": Tichy, *Buster Keaton*, p. 15.

39 "I appeared . . . before many different kinds": Kroszarski, *Hollywood Directors*, p. 145.

39 "In this knockabout act": Ibid., p. 151.

39 "One of the first things": Keaton, *My Wonderful World of Slapstick*, p. 13.

40 "If something tickled me": Blesh, *Keaton*, p. 40.

40 "*It is certain that Keaton's parents*": Ibid., p. 16.

Chapter 4

48   Then I thought of Kafka: Miller, *Thou Shalt Not Be Aware*, p. 242ff.

48   "Smilovitchi, the Lithuanian village": Forge, *Soutine*, p. 7.

51   I have often compared: Miller, *For Your Own Good*, p. 142ff.

52   A student has investigated: G. Bednarz, unpublished manuscript.

53–
54   The force of their message: Radström, *Hitlers Borndom*.

55   "Paul's father maintained": Chalfen, *Paul Celan*, pp. 36–38.

56   These were the witnesses: Miller, *Das verbannte Wissen*, chap. 2, sec. 2.

60   "led the life of a wastrel": Lawrin, *Fyodor M. Dostojevskij*, p. 9.

62   "The family of Joseph": Payne, *The Rise and Fall of Stalin*, p. 31.

63   "When Ekaterina Geladze married": Ibid., p. 32.

63   "The family of Stalin": Ibid., p. 33.

63   "According to Iremashvili": Ibid., p. 34.

64   "Church was a consolation": Ibid., p. 35.

64   "He was seven": Ibid., pp. 35–36.

PART TWO
Chapter 1

73   After having made this discovery: Miller, *Pictures of a Childhood*, p. 4.

73   and in the writings of Franz Kafka: Miller, *Thou Shalt Not Be Aware*, pp. 242–95.

79   "His father, when he had time": Janz, *Friedrich Nietzsche*, p. 48.

81   "upon leaving school": Ibid.

88   "Those who come across a book": Ibid., p. 10.

94   "One is an actor": Nietzsche, *Basic Writings of Nietzsche*, p. 629.

99   The documents I cite: Miller, *For Your Own Good*, p. 17ff.

101 The fact that this behavior: Miller, *Thou Shalt Not Be Aware*, pp. 87–88.

102 "I pursued the living": Nietzsche, *The Portable Nietzsche*, p. 226–228.

104 "With the storm": Ibid., p. 334.

105 "My heels twitched": Ibid., pp. 336–38.

106 "Is this today not the mob's?": Ibid., pp. 401–2.

107 "Do not let yourselves": Ibid., pp. 402–3.

108 "A free life is still free": Ibid., p. 163.

108 "If you would go high": Ibid., p. 402.

108 "For the terrible and almost": Nietzsche, *Werke*, vol. 4, p. 752.

108 "I don't believe I'm going to last": Deussen, *Erinnerungen an Friedrich Nietzsche*, p. 190.

111 "In Christianity the instincts": Nietzsche, *The Portable Nietzsche*, pp. 588–89.

112 "*hatred* of the natural": Ibid., p. 582.

112 "the expression of a profound vexation": Ibid., p. 582.

113 "If, for example, it makes men happy": Ibid., p. 591.

113 "So that it could say No": Ibid., p. 593.

114 "Psychologically considered": Ibid., p. 598.

114 "To repeat, I am against": Ibid., pp. 604–5.

115 "The concepts 'beyond' ": Ibid., pp. 611–12.

115 "In Paul the priest wanted power": Ibid., p. 618.

115 "The great lie of personal immortality": Ibid., pp. 618–19.

116 "The priest knows only": Ibid., pp. 629–30.

117 "When the herd animal": Nietzsche, *Basic Writings*, p. 786.

117 "False coasts and assurances": Ibid., pp. 785–86.

118 "The condition of the existence": Ibid., p. 785.

118 "Except for these ten-day works": Ibid., pp. 759–60.

120 "Light am I": Nietzsche, *The Portable Nietzsche*, pp. 217–18.

121 "How much truth does a spirit": Nietzsche, *Basic Writings*, pp. 674–75.

122 " 'God,' 'immortality of the soul' ": Ibid., p. 692–693.

123 "This ultimate, most joyous": Ibid., pp. 728–29.

123 "For a physiologist": Ibid., pp. 747–48.

124 "Luther, this calamity of a monk": Ibid., p. 776.

124 "The morality that would un-self": Ibid., pp. 789–91.

127 "It is necessary to say": Nietzsche, *The Portable Nietzsche*, p. 574.

127 "May I here venture": Nietzsche, *Basic Writings*, pp. 722–23.

128 "The Christian conception of God": Nietzsche, *The Portable Nietzsche*, pp. 585–86.

129 "When I wage war": Nietzsche, *Basic Writings*, p. 689.

130 Nor would it have been: Miller, *Das verbannte Wissen*, chap. 1, sec. 4; chap. 2, sec. 4.

132 As in the case of Kafka: Miller, *Thou Shalt Not Be Aware*, p. 307ff.

132 "When I seek my ultimate formula": Nietzsche, *Basic Writings*, p. 702.

PART THREE

Chapter 2

149 If this had not been so: Miller, *Das verbannte Wissen*, chap. 2, sec. 2.

150 "The Emperor's New Clothes": Andersen, *His Classic Fairy Tales*, pp. 119–124.

157 All that was needed: Leboyer, *Birth Without Violence*.

Appendix

167 Entire Appendix: From Miller, *For Your Own Good*.

Bibliography

ANDERSEN, HANS. *His Classic Fairy Tales*. Trans. Eric Haugaard. Illus. Michael Foreman. London, Gollancz, 1976.

BLESH, RUDI. *Keaton*. New York: Macmillan, 1966.

CHALFEN, ISRAEL. *Paul Celan: Eine Biographie seiner Jugend*. Frankfurt a. M.: Insel, 1983.

DEUSSEN, PAUL. *Erinnerungen an Friedrich Nietzsche*. Leipzig: Brockhaus, 1901.

FORGE, ANDREW. *Soutine*. London: Spring Books, 1965.

JANZ, CURT-PAUL. *Friedrich Nietzsche*. 3 vols. Munich: Hanser, 1978.

KEATON, BUSTER, with CHARLES SAMUELS. *My Wonderful World of Slapstick*. Garden City, N.Y.: Doubleday, 1960.

KOLLWITZ, HANS, ed. *The Diary and Letters of Käthe Kollwitz.* Trans. Richard and Clara Winston. Chicago: Henry Regnery, 1955.

KOLLWITZ, KÄTHE. *Ich sah die Welt mit liebevollen Blicken.* Wiesbaden: Fourier, 1983.

KROSZARSKI, RICHARD. *Hollywood Directors 1914–1940.* New York: Oxford Univ. Press, 1976.

LAWRIN, JANKO. *Fyodor M. Dostojevskij.* Reinbek: Rowohlt, 1963.

LEBOYER, FREDERICK. *Birth Without Violence.* London, Fontana, 1977.

MILLER, ALICE. *The Drama of Being a Child.* Trans. Ruth Ward. London, Virago, 1987.

————. *For Your Own Good: Hidden Cruelty in Child-rearing and the Roots of Violence.* Trans. Hildegarde and Hunter Hannum. London, Virago, 1987.

————. *Thou Shalt Not Be Aware: Society's Betrayal of the Child.* Trans. Hildegarde and Hunter Hannum. London, Pluto, 1986.

————. *Pictures of a Childhood: Sixty-six Watercolors and an Essay.* Trans. Hildegarde Hannum. New York: Farrar Straus, 1986.

————. *Das verbannte Wissen.* Frankfurt a. M.: Suhrkamp, 1988.

NIETZSCHE, FRIEDRICH. *Basic Writings of Nietzsche.* Translated and edited, with commentaries, by Walter Kaufmann. New York: Modern Library, 1968.

————. *The Portable Nietzsche.* Selected and translated, with an introduction, preface, and notes, by Walter Kaufmann. New York, Viking, 1954.

————. *Werke*. Ed. Karl Schlechta. 5 vols. Berlin and Vienna: Ullstein, 1972.

O'BRIAN, PATRICK. *Pablo Ruiz Picasso*. London, Collins, 1989.

PALAU I FABRE, JOSEP. *Picasso: The Early Years: 1881–1907*. Trans. Kenneth Lyons. London, Academy Editions, 1987.

PAYNE, ROBERT. *The Rise and Fall of Stalin*. New York: Simon and Schuster, 1965.

RADSTRÖM, NIKLAS. *Hitlers Borndom*. Stockholm: W & W, 1985.

SABARTÉS, JAIME. *Picasso: An Intimate Portrait*. Trans. Angel Flores. With eight Picasso reproductions. New York: Prentice-Hall, 1948.

TICHY, WOLFRAM. *Buster Keaton*. Reinbek: Rowohlt, 1983.

WIEGAND, WILFRIED. *Pablo Picasso*. Reinbek: Rowohlt, 1986.

Acknowledgments

Grateful acknowledgment is made to the following for permission to quote from previously published material:

Farrar, Straus & Giroux: Excerpt from *For Your Own Good* by Alice Miller. Copyright © 1983, 1984 by Alice Miller.

Doubleday: Excerpts from *His Classic Fairy Tales* by Hans Andersen, trans. Eric Haugaard. Copyright © 1978 by Doubleday, a division of Bantam Doubleday Dell Publishing Group, Inc.

Ediciones Poligrafa: Excerpts from *Picasso: The Early Years 1881–1907* by Palau i Fabre, trans. Kenneth Lyons. Copyright © 1981 by Rizzoli.

Verlag Gebr. Mann: Excerpts from *The Diary and Letters of Kaethe Kollwitz*, trans. Richard and Clara Winston. Copyright © 1955 by Henry Regnery, Chicago.

Carl Hanser Verlag: Excerpts from *Friedrich Nietzsche* by Curt-Paul Janz. Copyright © 1978 by Hanser.

Insel Verlag: Excerpts from *Paul Celan: Eine Biographie seiner Jugend* by Israel Chalfen. Copyright © 1983 by Insel.

The Literary Estate of Robert Payne: Excerpts from *The Rise and Fall of Stalin* by Robert Payne. Copyright © 1965 by Simon & Schuster.

Random House: Excerpts from *Basic Writings of Nietzsche*, translated and edited, with commentaries, by Walter Kaufmann. Copyright © 1966, 1967, 1968 by Random House, Inc. Reprinted by permission of the publisher.

Sterling Lord Literistic, Inc.: Excerpts from *My Wonderful World of Slapstick* by Buster Keaton. Reprinted by permission of Sterling Lord Literistic, Inc. Copyright © 1960 by Buster Keaton.

Viking Penguin: Excerpts from *The Portable Nietzsche*, trans. Walter Kaufmann. Copyright 1954 by the Viking Press, Inc. Copyright renewed © 1982 by Viking Penguin Inc. All rights reserved. Reprinted by permission of Viking Penguin, a division of Penguin Books USA, Inc.

Other Virago Books by Alice Miller

THE DRAMA OF BEING A CHILD

'Full of wisdom and perception' – Anthony Storr

'Every parent should read Alice Miller's *The Drama of Being a Child*. It might make for fewer casualties in that primal battlefield – the homestead'
– Edna O' Brien, *Observer*

'Illuminating and distressingly familiar. The reader has the complex experience of recognising a great truth simultaneously with revelation and the realisation of personal tragedy long and deeply suppressed'
– Ruth Rendell, *New Statesman*

Alice Miller's startling insights into child development are shared with us here as she explains her conviction that violence and cruelty in society have their roots in conventional child rearing and in education. She shows how many children, adapted from birth to the needs and ambitions of their parents, lose the ability to experience and express their true feelings, eventually to become estranged from their real selves. In sublimating their full potential in order to fulfil the desires of their parents, they impede the creativity, vitality and integrity that is authentically their own. Many people who have read her books have discovered within themselves the little child they once were. This may explain the strong and deep reactions Alice Miller's books have evoked in so many readers.

FOR YOUR OWN GOOD: THE ROOTS OF VIOLENCE IN CHILD-REARING

'She makes chillingly clear to the many what has been recognised only by the few: the extraordinary pain and psychological suffering inflicted on children under the guise of conventional child-rearing and pedagogy ... This book can change lives' – Maurice Sendak

'Child abuse is still sanctioned – indeed, held in high regard – in our society as long as it is defined as child-rearing. It is a tragic fact that parents beat their children in order to escape the emotions stemming from how they were treated by their own parents.'

Expanding on issues raised in her first book, *The Drama of Being a Child*, Dr Alice Miller here explores the sources of violence within ourselves and the way these are encouraged by orthodox child-rearing practices. Challenging the way in which we rationalise punishment and coercion as being for the child's 'own good', she illuminates the cost in compassion and humanity in later life, both in the private and public domain. Her message is clear: 'People whose integrity has not been damaged in childhood ... will feel no need to harm another person or themselves.'

BANISHED KNOWLEDGE:
FACING CHILDHOOD INJURIES

Alice Miller has achieved worldwide recognition for her work on the causes and effects of child abuse, on violence towards children and its cost to society. Her books have been international bestsellers. In *Banished Knowledge,* She writes:

'It is not true that evil, destructiveness, and perversion inevitably form part of human existence . . . But it is true that we are daily *producing* more evil . . . When one day the ignorance arising from childhood repression is eliminated and humanity has awakened, an end can be put to this production of evil.'

To eliminate her own repression, Alice Miller sought a therapy that would allow the injured child within the adult to find its own language, unimpeded by moral, pedagogic demands. After an exhaustive search, she found a method that withstood her scepticism and her dislike of dogma and salvational ideologies, enabling her to resolve the consequences of her own childhood traumas. Now she shares her knowledge with us. She believes that we can all, given sufficient motivation and instructions, follow her path: feel, and free, the banished child within us and, by letting that child speak, condemn the abuse and achieve liberation.